The Meaning of Life

Reid S. James, Ph.D

Copyright © 2013 Reid S. James, Ph.D
All rights reserved.

ISBN: 0615823173
ISBN 13: 9780615823171

Introduction

Ethics—the duties implied by ethics, and the rewards tied to it, have been a central issue with the human species simply because our species has advanced reasoning ability. Ethics and religion have always been tied together, for better or for worse. The Industrial Revolution didn't happen overnight nor was it achieved through the efforts of a single person, or even a few persons. The same with ethics—human ethics didn't happen overnight or through the efforts of a single person. This book is not really about the author creating much of anything in the area of ethics. In fact, the author is not personally equipped to do any such thing. I am a retired physiologist—not a trained philosopher nor trained theologian, nor even a trained sociologist. In short this book is not really any academic treatise on the subject, but rather an attempt simply to gather up many insights about ethics over human history and assemble them together much like one assembles a jig saw puzzle. Individual pieces of a jig saw puzzle don't tell us much about the big picture. If the pieces are put together correctly, a big picture emerges. And so it is the hope that I have put the pieces together reasonably well, well enough to give the readers food for thought.

The early chapters contain many quotations. These quotations are pieces of the puzzle, not included because I think they are always true, but because they pertain to the topic at hand. Some insights are hammered repetitiously because I didn't want to write a book in which the main points are lost amongst the clutter of minor points. Central to this book is the belief that human ethics is not dependent on academic degrees, religious titles, economic status, career choices, etc. Ethical people are found in all cultures, all kinds of economic groups, all kinds of career choices.

If I don't thank a small herd of people here it is because this topic is just one that has been with me for a lifetime, and only recently have I had the desire to put all the pieces together. Every author of every quote is to be thanked because their pioneer efforts made it possible for the pieces of this puzzle to exist for assemblage.

All those a part of my life at some point, in the formative, productive, and terminational phases, influenced the context of this book. I need especially to thank the proof-reader—Judith P. Edwards—for her conscientious effort to make the content grammatically correct. When it comes to placing quotation marks properly, any variation is due to my own intransigence regarding this matter.

Each of us has a peculiar history and but a brief time to exist in the evolutionary process. Certainly my own peculiar history brings with it some bias ("I am part of all that I have met", Alfred Lord Tennyson, English Poet). And all readers will bring their own peculiar biases to the topic. But in the end, with every ensuing generation, a clearer understanding of the topic will bring about a new consensus about the nature of ethics. It isn't just the physical aspects of evolution which change over time, but conceptual matters as well. Thus, whatever this book is, it is not a final word about anything.

About the Author

I am a retired Physiologist. It is well enough to say I am retired with time enough to sit and think. Sometimes I just sit. If surviving to the age of retirement is an accomplishment, then let that be the sum of it. Any other particulars about me are irrelevant to this book. Seeking meaning to life is not limited to trained philosophers or clergy. Nor is such a task likely to be achieved without the valued input from so many others—others whose thoughts add so much more depth to the topic.

I have an undergraduate degree in Biology from Bates College, a Master's Degree in Physiology from the Univ. of Wisconsin, and a Ph.D. degree in Physiology from the Univ. of Wisconsin.

Chapter 1

I hazard a conjecture that most everyone ponders the meaning of life. It is one of those questions which, in the end, challenges our mental capacity. Where did 'all this' come from and what does it all mean? In one form or another most of us attribute 'all of this' as a creation by God. I myself simplify this frustrating question by reasoning that for every gift there must be a gift giver. Thus, 'all of this' came from God via His created process of evolution. We do know quite a bit about the evolutionary process and it is, by far, the greatest and most astonishing process imaginable. But still, no matter how we slice it, the question then becomes, "Where did God come from?" Here is where human mental acumen hits the stone wall. Something had to come from nothing. By definition this is impossible. Thus, there is a dimension of reality beyond our capacity to comprehend—so far. There is no logical reason to believe this God created evolutionary process is completed or near completed, or our human species is the final evolutionary touchdown, 'the creme de la creme' of evolved species.

(1) Relevant Attestations:

The best summary supporting evolution as fact, not belief, is the book "<u>The Greatest Show on Earth</u>" by Richard Dawkins (English ethologist, evolutionary biologist, and author)

"God is a circle whose center is everywhere and whose circumference is nowhere". Empedocies (Greek philosopher)

But be all this as it may, what role do each of us play, and how can we live a meaningful life? I don't know why anyone my age would waste time analyzing this; it seems kind of late to get hung up on this question. Of course this has been a question for most of us all our lives. I can remember as a kid sitting on a hillside with my pet dog Buff and asking him, "What the hell are we both in this life for?" His analysis was simple: "Let's play." And for him that may well have been an excellent answer. If he could have the right owner and live in the right situation he would play and eat himself to one happy tune until death—death being an event which would never have crossed his mind. But nothing is that simple for humans. Our forte in this evolutionary hierarchy is to possess an advanced ability to reason, coupled with an inherent sense of ethics. Both of these represent potentials, varying in degree, and need to be developed and practiced. Both, I suspect, play a huge role in meaningful human existence.

Many philosophers use the word happiness as the goal which gives meaning to our lives. I prefer the word contentment. I can be happy my team won a game, but that doesn't make my life contented. And, of course, no one can be contented all the time. If I got a traffic ticket no one would say I was contented at the time. Still, the word is useful. There are some times in life when we are more content than others. In my case, I probably am more contented now than at any time earlier in my life. BUT, I also have no regrets about the times earlier when life was more complicated, more challenging, more stressful, more mysterious, more frustrating. There is a lot to be said for the exhilaration of so many varied experiences in life. The tumult may have been greater, but so were the highs of successes. We all prefer not to die, **BUT**—if we did live forever it would be the same old-same old, over and over. As I said before, the God-created evolutionary process is truly amazing. The first time one accomplishes something is always more rewarding than the next time, and to get the same high as originally, some sort of 'extra' has to be added. The first time you win a race is really exciting. In the future, to get the same sort of high in winning the race, you need to better your time or set a record or beat someone you dislike, and so on. At some point there is nothing more to be added on and, in fact, as one's skills decline in a specific venture, you have to let go and find some other avenue for success, or discontent with one's life will set in. There are so many mountains to climb in life, and yet, every time, we discover that, after we get to the top, the next step is always downhill—sometimes it may even be a cliff after which comes a free fall. So we peak, we stagnate or fall, and we pick ourselves up with new challenges. Till death the race never ends.

To me, according to my conceptual perceptions, the first step toward achieving contentment is a realization that everything in life is impermanent. **CHANGE** is the operative word in the evolutionary process. People who resist change are never the happiest campers in life. What is there around us that is really etched in stone? Very little. Friendships often don't last forever, marriages may not, a job may not, health won't, physical skills don't, sexual drives don't, and so on. I always have to stifle a laugh when clergy say in a marriage ceremony, "What God has put together let no man put asunder." If God is really arranging marriages He must be perceptually deficient. Development, Change, and Loss are the engines which pull our train through life.

In fact, some of those least contented in life have inherited certain religious dogmas/beliefs, and on faith accept them as fact; and then with their God on their side, they really cannot stand all the heathens around them. It seems rather silly for anyone to have such a self-serving notion that inherited religion is God's way of communicating with us, that God made us in His image, that God is personally involved with us as individuals, that God needs our prayers in order to do some good thing, that God would use a prayer of ours to super-cede His laws which govern the process of evolution, and that if we go through certain rituals we will be granted entrance to heaven. Clearly this is all extremely self serving **ALBEIT** understandable. People fear death, as expected, and, natural as it is, they want to believe there is life after death. For all I know maybe there is, but it is a belief, and no amount of faith can make it a fact. The problem is, such blind faith **PREVENTS CONTENTMENT.** It prevents contentment **BECAUSE** our whole lives will be filled with disappointments as God fails us—I mean, we prayed so hard, we went to the right church and went through all the rituals, and put money in the collection plate, and yet just as many bad things happen to us as anybody else, of course more or less on a random basis. The only way to rationalize God's failure to be our true friend and protect us from all of life's booby traps, is to desperately rationalize vaguely that God operates in mysterious ways, throw up our hands and try to repair our hurt feelings. I suppose, if we really feel we are being rejected or ignored by God, we ought to feel a bit depressed. So we desperately regroup: maybe we are not zealous enough in going after all the heathens on the planet, or at least in our own life community. We maybe need to be better religious warriors to get to heaven. Dead soldiers are rarely bereft of religious clergy of some sort blessing them for their bravery in a 'just' war. Each side, in every war, is always buttressed by clergy of this or that ilk, and of course has God on its side. Either God is two-faced and a sadist, or God doesn't use inherited religion as the method to spread His directives.

I came, over time, to realize that religious faith-based fervor over inherited religion is not a way to live a contented life. For the most part, I don't even find it particularly pleasant to be around people who have this type of belief. Most of them are always angry about something, upset about others, very intolerant of others, inflexible in their thinking, full of imagined moral superiority, and seem to go through life with their heads up their ass most of the time. There can be no reasoned discussion with them about religion or their politics because both are faith based, and if called upon to explain any particulars about their faith based notions they invariably respond, "I don't want to talk about it". These same people have another favorite expression: "I can't stand _____." You can fill in the person or custom or dress code, etc. They really can't stand an awful lot of people or things and clearly are not contented souls. "Saved souls," they would insist, but for now they hardly are a contented lot. Contentment for them will have to wait for Heaven.

(2) Relevant Attestations:

"Prayer: To ask that the rules of the Universe be annulled on behalf of a single petitioner, confessedly unworthy." Ambrose Bierce (U.S. writer)

"The great writers to whom the world owes what religious liberty it possesses, have mostly asserted freedom of conscience as an indefeasible right, and denied absolutely that a human being is accountable to others for his religious belief. Yet so natural to mankind is intolerance in whatever they really care about, that religious freedom has hardly anywhere been practically realized." John Stuart Mill (English political economist, philosopher).

"It is not so much God who created Man in His own image, as every one of us who creates unto himself a God in his own image." Unknown.

"There is no argument in the world that carries the hatred that a religious belief one does." Will Rodgers (American cowboy, comedian, social commentator)

So then, what kind of life is to be lived in order to have a contented life here on earth? It starts with understanding and accepting that we don't go through life on a level playing field or earn many of the attributes or environments which will enable us to more easily achieve a contented life. I suppose we can believe that God directed a specific sperm to a specific egg so that on purpose **WE** exist or **HITLER** comes to exist. Or we are born in America in a nice neighborhood with good parents at the right time in American history because God so willed it. Well, if God did, it certainly cannot be because we earned this good fate. We didn't. We haven't even lived yet. Of course those born in a drug house to a crack mother in downtown Newark did not earn their fate either. Of course they didn't. And I doubt we really want to believe God personally created Hitler. Chance, survival of the fittest, and change are the operative laws of God's created evolutionary process. What each of us have gotten is a chance, by chance, with certain genetics, by chance, to be born in an environment, by chance. When the cards are dealt in a poker game we are given a chance to win. Of course we, with our minds of 'free will', have a chance to play our cards well or poorly. In this sense much of our lives are not simple fate or destiny, but filled with opportunities to become more contented. Is it possible to be born with a genetic make-up that simply closes the door to a contented life? Maybe it is. If you are born with severe genetic defects—no limbs, blind, deaf, and any other myriad such combinations perhaps a contented life is not possible. Is it even ethical to bring such an embryo to term? One thing seems obvious: if God created the laws which govern evolution this genetic misfortune was not planned by God in any personal way. There are successes and tragedies throughout the entire evolutionary process. Nothing about evolution is centered around individuals of any species. If any of us wants to feel important in this phenomenon of life, we need find another planet and another process. That we cannot be center stage, cuddled by God, and be protected and guided to have a great life does not mean, therefore, that we cannot achieve some contentment with our lives. And we certainly won't if we insist that, absent this kind of personal involvement with God, we cannot be contented. These faith-based religious fundamentalists are so fearful of death that they fail to realize evolution has gone on now for millions of years without them. Can't they just be grateful they won a lottery and have the chance to be a short term participant in the process? There is nothing to fear from death; I mean do we have nightmares about those millions of years when we did not exist? Of course we don't. I don't. So why should you or I have nightmares about a time when we may not exist again, ever? Why do so many people have to put all this in terms of heaven and hell? What kind of sadistic God do they worship anyway who torments people, threatens them, picks certain nations to be His flock, and then sends them to be tortured in a hell for their inability to please Him? Or insists someone has to die for us to be saved? There was a time when this kind of scary nonsense prevailed and we had the Inquisition and all the gruesome tortures that went with it. Remnants of this are still found in the belief that the death penalty deters crime.

You know, if going to hell doesn't scare someone I can't imagine why the death penalty would. Logic necessitates my adding one caveat here: Since we cannot at some level understand life as we now know it, there is of course a possibility that a life hereafter, beyond our comprehension could still exist. It is just hard to envision God whispering in certain ears assuring heaven, for them, is just around the corner.

We could, I guess, tolerate non-contentment here in life because after death, we will be contented for evermore. The ultimate meaning of life then, becomes to die, under the grace of God, so that contentment can begin. But why then is it the religious right who so desperately want to prolong a life, any kind of life, as long as possible, even if the person in question has had enough? Don't they want that person to hurry up and get to heaven? I remember being trapped in a hospital room with a poor guy, a member of the clergy, who had had a severe stroke and was completely paralyzed except for blinking his eyes. His flock would come by and say, "God is not done with you yet". Am I really to believe it is God who is toying with this guy like a cat might do with a mouse before the final kill? I find all this beyond absurdity and extremely sadistic. If anything is personal, the dying process is, and every person should be able to control their dying process, at the time, or via advance directives. When I have had enough, it would be really nice if all the religious narcissists could be kept at bay. Let them die a drawn out painful, useless ordeal if they want, but I just wish hundreds of thousands of dollars spent on allowing them to do this could be spent on those younger people with a useful life ahead. Both my parents lived long useful independent lives; both in their last years wanted to die, grateful for the good life they had been fortunate enough to live, and yet both feared God would be displeased if they endorsed their own deaths. This may not have been the case with my father; I kind of suspect he arranged with his doctor not to get treatment which would prolong his life. How much nicer it would have been if he could have been open about it and all of us who were close to him could have been there to let him leave life in a comfortable, supportive, pleasant way. Treating death as a catastrophe adds another stumbling block to contentment while living.

(3) Relevant Attestations:

"It matters not how a man dies, but how he lives. The act of dying is not of importance, it lasts so short a time." Samuel Johnson (British Lexicographer)

"No one can walk backward into the future." Hoseph Hergesheimer (American writer)

"Man….is born without his own consent; his organization does in no wise depend on himself; his ideas come to him involuntarily; his habits are in the power of those who cause him to contract them; his unceasingly modified by causes whether visible or concealed, over which he has no control; which necessarily regulate his mode of existence, give the hue to his way of thinking, and determine his manner of acting. He is good or bad, happy or miserable, wise or foolish, reasonable or irrational, without his will being for any thing in their various states…..Nevertheless….it is pretended he is a free agent, or……determines his own will, and regulates his own condition." Paul Henri Thiry, Caron D'holbach (French materialist philosopher)

"Say nothing of my religion. It is known to God and myself alone. Its evidence before the world is to be sought in my life: if it has been honest and dutiful to society the religion which has regulated it cannot be a bad one." Thomas Jefferson (President, U.S.)

"The death of dogma is the birth of reality." Immanuel Kant (German philosopher)

"Faith in immortality, like belief in God, leaves unanswered the ancient question: is God unable to prevent suffering, and thus not omnipotent? or is he able and not willing it and thus not merciful? And is he just?" Walter Kaufmann (American philosopher)

"The wise man looks at death with honesty, dignity and calm, recognizing that the tragedy it brings is inherent in the great gift of life." Corless Lamont (American philosopher)

"New times demand new measures and new men;
The world advances, and in time outgrows
The laws which in our 'fathers' day were best." James Russell Lowell (American Poet)

"The end of life would be much less frightening if it were not called death any more. The fear of death is the source of all religions." Maurice Maeterlinck (Belgian dramatist)

"The fact that an opinion has been widely held is no evidence that it is not utterly absurd; indeed in view of the silliniess of the majority of mankind, a widespread belief is more often likely to be foolish than sensible." Bertrand Russell (British mathematician, philosopher)

"A man who is good for anything ought not to calculate the chance of living or dying; he ought only to consider whether in doing anything he is doing right or wrong–acting the part of a good man or a bad....for the fear of death is indeed the pretense of wisdom, and not real wisdom, but a pretense of knowing the unknown; and no one knows whether death, which men in their fear apprehend to be the greatest evil, may not be the greatest good." Socrates (Greek general, philosopher)

"In the long run we are all dead." John Maynard Keynes (British economist)

"All our knowledge merely helps us to die a more painful death than the animals what know nothing." Maurice Maeterlinck (Belgian Poet)

"Death is more universal than life; everyone dies but not everyone lives." A. Sachs (Israel Scholar)

"I wouldn't live forever,
I wouldn't if I could;
But I needn't fret about it.
For I couldn't if I would." Unknown

"The worst deluded are the self-deluded. C.N. Bovee (19th century author)

"Man's life's a vapor,
And full of woes;
He cuts a caper,
And down he goes." Unknown

"Let us give thanks, not only for what we have but for what we have escaped." Unknown

"Once I wasn't
Then I was
Now I ain't again" Unknown

"Every man desires to live long, but no man would be old." Jonathan Swift (Anglo Irish satirist and essayist)

"What is an individual man? An atom, almost invisible without a magnifying glass—a mere speck upon the surface of the immense universe; not a second in time, compared to immeasurable, never-beginning, and never ending eternity; a drop of water in the great deep, which evaporates and is borne off by the winds; a grain of sand, which is soon gathered to the dust from which it sprung." Henry Clay (American lawyer, politician, orator)

"If history teaches anything, it teaches self-delusion in the face of unpleasant facts is folly." Ronald Reagan (Actor, American President)

Chapter 2

Where are we so far with this 'meaning of life' question? What, we need to ask, is the purpose of human life? We know the purpose of a knife—it is to be sharp to cut things. I suppose the purpose of all living forms of life is to be part of God's created evolutionary process. But this overall view of human purpose is too generalized. Humans differ from other species primarily in their ability to reason, to remember, to be ethical, and to laugh. The dog-eat-dog mentality phase of evolutionary development is more characteristic of lower forms of life. It would seem, therefore, that contentment must derive from humans doing what humans have the potential to do best: to use ethics as the basis for our behavior; to remember the past in order to learn from our mistakes, and to use humor/laughter to reduce the stresses of our lives. No matter what the distinguishing capabilities of differing species, these characteristics vary amongst the different members of the species. Thus, the ability to reason or to be ethical is not the same, but varies amongst humans. Genetics and personal environment complicate the issues here. Faith based inherited religious dogma, standing alone, clearly does not lead to a contented life. Also, some lives are so overpowered by genetic or environmental circumstances that contentment, if achievable at all, may be substantially limited.

In lower animals, the chips fall where they may, and the fittest survive and evolution moves forward. With humans, **BECAUSE OF OUR ETHICAL NATURE**, there is an obligation to help the less fortunate have a more level playing field, to enable the less fortunate to achieve some level of contentment. Ethics is all about obligation.

It is reason which leads all human societies to understand the validity of the Golden Rule. Because we are human—able to use reason as the basis for ethics—we understand the Golden Rule; all people everywhere understand it. Only those with a psychopathic mental condition cannot tell right from wrong almost all the time. We know, for example, that it is only fair we spend the same amount of money to educate all children. We know this. It is the fair way. There is no logical reason why certain children should be favored here. And this kind of ethical reasoning can be applied to the vast majority of issues.

IF WE CANNOT LIVE UP TO OUR POTENTIAL as humans, a potential which varies from human to human, it does not seem a high level of contentment can be achieved. We can proceed full steam ahead with self-serving goals of power, wealth, titles, materialism, hedonistic addictions of varied sorts—and cloak all of this in some sort of inherited religious faith based delusions, **BUT—** personal contentment will be nothing more than fleeting moments of surreal bouts of happiness which, even while they happen, are supplanted by the need for a stronger replay requiring even more power, wealth, titles, materialism, or hedonistic addiction. None of this is real contentment. It is these 'addictions' which override our ethical nature, which then require us to invent faith-based notions of justifiability for why we do not act ethically. We can all do this, and **WE ALL DO**, to varying degrees, but contentment is not achieved by rationalizing our actions.

We can wrap ourselves up in concepts like family values and live a life in which it is we and those within our own family who serve as our focus for daily actions. The wagons are circled, and others become enemies or at least irrelevant. Everything becomes 'what is best for us and our kind'—a reversion to survival of the fittest.

Many philosophers have concluded that those who do not 'serve' others cannot live contented lives. And the 'others' cannot be just our own family or ourselves, or particular groups of which we may be a part. Diversity is the means whereby God's evolutionary process moves forward, so by definition diversity is good. So here we have it—**DIVERSITY IS GOOD AND ETHICS IS A SPECIES OBLIGATION**. If a knife is not sharp, it is not a good knife, it is not serving the purpose for which it exists. If we fail to develop our ethical potential or use reason for our daily decisions, daily plans/conceptual beliefs—then we cannot be considered personally successful, and without this personal success in developing our species potential, achieving contentment will be limited.

Evolution is most often viewed from the changes in physical characteristics as life forms move up the animal and plant kingdoms. But there have been huge social and behavioral changes too. That humans have the ability to laugh, have advanced reasoning powers, and have a sense of ethics is especially noteworthy. No one claims they got their sense of humor via some sort of inherited dogma about how to laugh. We seldom claim our ability to reason was achieved via some sort of inherited dogma about the proper way to reason. **AND YET**, the origin of our ethical nature is often claimed to come from inherited religious dogma. To me, this is irrational. **A REMARKABLE ASPECT OF OUR SPECIES IS OUR ABILITY TO UNDERSTAND THE GOLDEN RULE.** No longer is the 'good life' available only to those most 'fit' (genetics). While degrees of contentedness vary, as every other genetic variation does, with humans there is an advanced capability to create a more level playing field so that others, too, can achieve some contentedness in their lives. This duty for generosity and stewardship is not limited to just other humans, but to other species as well, and toward the natural resources of our planet. Clearly this evolving responsibility is not perfected, and may yet, another time around in evolutionary history, succeed after a huge evolutionary upheaval.

The meaning of life is found by not missing the forest for the sake of the trees. The meaning of life is found by actively attempting to 'fit in' with God's created evolutionary process—to go with the flow, so to speak, with this process of which we are but a transitory part. Of course we prefer this process be centered around ourselves, that God be our personal friend, our personal protector, our personal path to contentment. There is no evidence of this whatsoever, and thus any such self-serving notions have to be faith-based beliefs. Our 'free will' entitles us to believe anything we want, but willy-nilly wispy beliefs, inherited or otherwise, are not facts, and no amount of faith can make them so. Thus, to put all this in the largest over-all perspective: only our species' inherent ability to reason and behave ethically permit contentment to be achieved, which is the real goal and meaning for our lives as human beings.

(4) Relevant Attestations:

"Integrity without knowledge is weak and useless, and knowledge without integrity is dangerous and dreadful." Samuel Johnson (British Lexicographer)

"Let us have faith that right makes might; and in that faith let us to the end, dare to do our duty as we understand it." Abraham Lincoln (U.S. President)

"Stupidity does not consist in being without ideas. Such stupidity would be the sweet, blissful stupidity of animals, molluscs and the gods. Human stupidity consists in having lots of ideas, but stupid ones." Henry de Monthelant (French novelist)

"It is the tragedy of the world that no one knows what he doesn't know—and the less man knows, the more sure he is that he knows everything." Joyce Cary (British novelist)

"To say that a blind custom of obedience should be a surer obligation than duty taught and understood....is to affirm that a blind man may tread surer by a guide than a seeing man by a light." Francis Bacon (English essayist, philosopher)

"I am arguing that science can, in principle, help us understand what we should do and should want—and therefore, what other people should do and should want in order to live the best lives possible." Sam Harris (neuroscientist)

"If the basic claims of religion are true, the scientific worldview is so blinkered and susceptible to supernatural modification as to be rendered nearly ridiculous; if the basic claims of religion are false, most people are profoundly confused about the nature of reality, confounded by irrational hopes and fears, and tending to waste precious time and attention—often with tragic results." Sam Harris (neuroscientist)

"There are in fact four very significant stumbling-blocks in the way of grasping the truth, which hinder every man however learned, and scarcely allow anyone to win a clear title to wisdom, namely, the example of weak and unworthy authority, long standing custom, the feeling of the ignorant crowd, and the hiding of our own ignorance while making a display of our apparent knowledge." Roger Bacon (English philosopher, scientist)

"Wisdom, compassion and courage—these are the three universally recognized moral qualities of men." Confucius (Chinese Sage, philosopher)

"In the long run of history, the censor and the inquisitor have always lost. The only sure weapon against bad ideas is better ideas. The source of better ideas is wisdom. The surest path to wisdom is a liberal education." Alfred Whitney Griswold (President of Yale)

"The less men reason, the more wicked they are. Savages, princes, nobles, and dregs of the people, are commonly the worst of men, because they reason least." Paul Henri Thiry, Baron D'holbach (French materialist, philosopher)

"A new scientific truth does not triumph by convincing its opponents and making them see the light, but rather because its opponents eventually die out, and a new generation grows up that is familiar with it." Max Planck (Originator of the Quatum Theory)

"Advance or decadence are the only choices offered to mankind. The pure conservative is fighting against the essence of the universe." Alfred North Whitehead (British mathematician, philosopher)

"Facts do not cease to exist because they are ignored." Aldous Huxley (English Writer)

"If we want life, we must conquer darkness." J. T. Fields (American editor, publisher, and poet)

"Truth uttered before it's time is always dangerous." Mencius (Chinese Philosopher)

"The reasoning goes as follows: I want, and if I want something I need it; if I need it, I have a right to it; if I have a right to it, someone else has an obligation to provide it." Dr. John Cova, Consultant to the Health Insurance Industry)

"The religious right is neither." Ephemera Buttons

"None is so blind as he who will not see." Unknown

"An ignorant democracy leads directly to war." Eilihu Root (American politician)

"Real intelligence consists not so much in knowing how to do what you have learned to do, but in knowing how to behave in circumstances for which no prior experience has prepared you." Sydney Harris (Essayist and Drama Critic)

"The principles now implanted in thy bosom will grow, and one day reach maturity; and in that maturity thou wilt find thy Heaven or thy Hell." D. Thomas (American Agricultural writer)

"The essence of knowledge is, having it, to apply it: not having it, to confess your ignorance." Confucius (Chinese Philosopher)

"It is better to be vaguely right than precisely wrong." Sydney Harris (American essayist and drama critic)

"Any fool can make a rule and every fool will mind it." Unknown

Chapter 3

With this overall perspective in place, the devil, as always, is in the details. We may be born with all sorts of potentials in varied human traits, but there is often a huge disconnect between what we say we understand or believe, and what our actions portray. An imagined good Christian, for example, would take issue with my negative comments about inherited religious beliefs. For instance, I have been asked if I have ever read the Bible, have I ever believed in Christ, etc. The answer is yes and yes. I also believe Buddha was a moral person, the Dalai Lama is a moral person, Gandhi was a moral person, etc. The 'prophets' who founded the major religions of the day were ethically admirable individuals—but human, and therefore not perfect. I admire those who act out the beliefs these prophets preached. BUT, most Christians and other sectarians don't even come close. Can anyone seriously read the Bible and believe Christ would support establishing military bases all over the globe, attacking Vietnam as we did, supporting political policies which enable 2-5% of citizens to own 90% of the wealth, to be against spending the same amount of money to educate all children, oppose enforcing responsible reproduction in order to save the planet from the devastation caused by human overpopulation, oppose policies which protect natural resources/other species, etc.? The list goes on and on. If people actually followed the principles upon which their religion was based, it **WOULD BE** an ethical world. **OF COURSE THEY DON'T**. Also, none of these prophets wrote scripture. If these written scriptures are God's mechanism to convey ethical dictates, why would they be written by others from memory many decades after a prophet dies? Finally, if these scriptures are actual 'words' from God, would they not be perfect for generations to come in every detail? Yet they are not—all scriptures written so long ago have obvious inaccuracies because of the ignorance prevalent at the time they were written. For these reasons lie my negativity towards inherited religions. This is not to deny that some people actually do follow the principles of the prophets, who founded their religion, and I doubt they would find much wrong with anything I write here. They would be more dismayed as to the state of the religion they practice.

Contentment is derived from the use of our innate reasoning, and from our innate sense of ethics to help others to be treated with more justice. Education supplies the data from which we base our reasoning. The universal Golden Rule—the basis for ethics——supplies the support needed to effectuate a more level playing field for all of humanity. If we do not use reason to understand the laws which govern God's created evolutionary process, then we are missing knowledge to understand the nature of life itself. If we do not understand, at some level, the physiology of our own body, we cannot protect our health properly. In the absence of our understanding the evolutionary process and all the parts of that process, we will gravitate to self-delusion about the importance of ourselves in the process, viewing diversity of life as a threat rather than appreciating the role diversity plays in the whole process. **TO ACHIEVE CONTENTMENT WE NEED TO**

COME TO GRIPS WITH DEATH, a most natural and inevitable part of our life. To fear what we cannot change, what cannot hurt us, is irrational and generates many of the self serving delusional human behaviors. To have an army of clergy preaching it is life after death which is the meaning of life, that God communicates to us through clergy, that failure to follow the dogmas of our inherited or adopted-through-marriage religion will result in some sort of hell after death, hardly provides the basis for reaching contentment in our lives. **EVERYONE NEEDS TO HAVE BELIEFS**, as reason often is absent the facts, **BUT BELIEFS NEED TO BE RATIONAL**, believable, fit the available evidence, and **FIT THE GOLDEN RULE**. Without developing our ethical capability, contentment is illusive and ephemeral. People who go through life with braces on their brains are robotic, obsessed with ritualistic habits, fearful of diversity, suspicious and non-supportive of others different from themselves.

This may reflect simply a personal quirk, but I sense it is hard to understand the meaning of life without one's becoming close to nature itself, in some form or fashion. Nothing grounds my own thoughts or emotions more than my solitary wandering around in nature settings and urban streets. **TO COMMUNE IN SOME WAY WITH NATURE BRINGS THE TOTAL PICTURE OF LIFE INTO PLAY**—otherwise we miss the forest for the sake of the trees. It is easy to spend too much of life on little things, to sweat the small stuff; in the end, most of it is small stuff. The real process of evolution is not a Walt Disney sort of event; anything controlled by genetics, chance, diversity, environment, and luck is not exactly going to be a 'zip-a-dee do dah day', 'tip toe through the tulips', 'Alice in Wonderland' experience. **BIRTH GIVES EVERY NEW PLAYER IN THE EVOLUTIONARY PROCESS A CHANCE.** Period. It is the presence of an ethical nature in humans which **ENABLES** the less fortunate to have a greater **CHANCE** to achieve contentment. Ethics, by its very nature, implies DUTY. **TO FAIL IN OUR INHERENT ETHICAL RESPONSIBILITIES IS TO STUNT THE ACHIEVEMENT OF PERSONAL CONTENTMENT IN LIFE.** People who seek personal contentment via wealth, power, titles, sex, and all other such ilk, will find nothing but momentary surges of satisfaction, just enough to keep driving them onwards in the same mode, ever trying to achieve meaningful contentment. But it will never come. The nature of all addictions and obsessions is to require even more of the same to achieve the same high and every high is followed by succeeding higher bouts of depression. This, we call, the **RAT RACE**. One can implant an electrode into a certain area of a rat's brain which will cause the rat to hit a lever constantly to get food until the rat eats itself to death. You can call this pleasure, if you want, because the rat never stops hitting the bar to get more food, but **OBSESSIVE BEHAVIOR IS NEVER CONTENTMENT**. Contentment is the goal, not purposeless achievement of power, food, titles, wealth, sex, winning contests, etc.

(5) Relevant Attestations:

"Not all that tempts your wand'ring eyes
And heedless hearts, is lawful prize;
Nor all that glitters, gold." Thomas Gray (British Poet)

"I have learned to look on nature, not as in the hour
Of thoughtless youth; but hearing often-times
The still sad music of humanity." William Wordsworth (British Poet)

"The world is too much with us, late and soon,
Getting and spending, we lay waste our powers;

Little we see in Nature that is ours." Willaim Wordsworth (British Poet)

"When a small child....I thought success spelled happiness. I was wrong. Happiness is like a butterfly which appears and delights us for one brief moment, but soon flits away." Anna Pavlova (Russian Ballet dancer)

"The more a man lays stress on false possessions, and the less sensitivity he has for what is essential, the less satisfying is his life." Carl Gustav Jung (Swiss psychologist, psychiatrist)

"Christendom has done away with Christianity, without being aware of it. Therefore, if anything is to be done about it, the attempt must be made to reintroduce Christianity." Soren Kierkegaard (Danish theologian)

"The greatest wealth is to live content with little, for there is never want where the mind is satisfied." Lucretius (Roman Poet)

"You'll be old and you never lived, and you kind of feel silly to lie down and die and to never have lived, to have been a job chaser and never have lived." Gertrude Stein (American writer)

"Look at one of your industrious fellows for a moment. He sows hurry and reaps indigestion; he puts a vast deal of activity out to interest, and receives a large measure of nervous derangement in return....I do not care how much or how well he works, this fellow is an evil feature in other people's lives. They would be happier if he were dead...He poisons life at the well-head." Robert Louis Stevenson (British essayist, novelist, poet).

"Success, a sort of suicide, is ruined by success." Edward Young (English Poet)

"Wealth, after all, is a relative thing, since he that has little, and wants less, is richer than he that has much, and wants more." C. C. Colton (English Cleric and Writer)

"The mass of men lead lives of quiet desperation." Henry David Thoreau. (American author, philosopher, abolitionist, naturalist, surveyor, historian, transcendentalist)

"Going to church doesn't make you a Christian any more than going to the garage makes you a car. Laurence J. Peter." (Educator, author of Peter Principle)

"Incompetence is vanity and PR and people who talk about 'massaging' or positioning' or 'spin control'. It's a society that celebrates style over substance, image over reality, credentials over experience; a society that embraces the credo of the Philadelphia sheriff John Green—'Fake it till you make it'; a society devoted to consuming and acquiring, to self-fulfillment and self-indulgence, a society infatuated with money, power, sex, and drugs; a narcissistic, solipsistic, materialistic society saturated with advertising, dominated by entertainment, and living only for the here and now." Art Carey (American editor and author)

"Strip away the clothes and polish, and many of today's white collar outlaws are just as amoral and unrepentant as 'wilding' ghetto kids. Their business ethic is the legal principle 'innocent until proven guilty'. Do whatever it takes to boost profits and make millions and protect your plunder, because, no matter how damnable your behavior, you've done nothing wrong until you're caught and convicted. And then, of course, it's not really your fault, it's the fault of the 'system', it's the fault of society, it's the fault of the economy, it's the fault of overzealous prosecutors, it's the fault of loosely written laws and poorly policed regulations that made wrong-doing too tempting to resist. Art Carey (American editor and author)

"In our complex, modern world....large private fortunes can easily be extracted by clever folks through imaginative zero sum or negative-sum games. You may become engineers, physicians, or product entrepreneurs who earn your income as a reward for contributing to the welfare and prosperity of society as a whole....On the other hand, you may join the ever-growing corps of income redistributors—tax experts, legal experts, regulatory experts, financial wizards, lobbyists, legislators, and so on—who use so much of their time and intellect not to create net social value added, but merely to redistribute toward themselves and their clients claims to the useful production of others." Uwe E. Reinhardt (Princeton Economist)

"Unfortunately, in our eagerness to embrace diversity and pluralism, to erase all the isms of the past, to be tolerant, sensitive, and nonjudgemental, we have created a new secular religion. It's name is Openness, and its fundamental dogma is an unqualified acceptance of anybody and everybody, anything and everything. All moral judgements are strictly subjective; right or wrong, good or bad; it's all in the eye of the perpetrator." Art Carey (American author and editor)

"The trouble with the rat race is that even if you win, you're still a rat." Unknown

"I am richer than E. H. Harriman, I have all the money I want and he hasn't." John Muir (American Naturalist)

"First I was dying to finish high school and start college
And then I was dying to finish college and start working
And then I was dying for my children to grow old enough for school so I could return to work
And then I was dying to retire
And now, I am dying......and suddenly I realize I forgot to live." Unknown

"The most worthwhile form of education is the kind that puts the educator inside you, as it were, so that the appetite for learning persists long after the external pressure for grades and degrees has vanished. Otherwise you are not educated; you are merely trained." Sydney Harris (American Essayist and Drama Critic)

"I have to live with myself, and so
I want to be fit for myself to know;
I want to be able as days go by,
Always to look myself straight in the eye." Edgar A. Guest (English born American poet)

"Youth is a period of building up in habits, and hopes, and faiths--not an hour but is trembling with destinies; not a moment, once passed, of which the appointed work can ever be done again, or the neglected blows struck on the cold iron.....by all means sometimes be alone; salute thyself; see what they soul doth wear; dare to look in they chest, and tumble up and down what thou findest there...for the principles now implanted in thy bosom will grow, and one day reach maturity; and in that maturity thou wilt find they heaven or they hell." Unknown

"We dwell in times of great perplexity and are beset by far-reaching problems of social, industrial, and political import..... We shall not greatly err if upon every occasion we consult the genius of Abraham Lincoln. We shall not falter nor swerve from the path of national righteousness if we live by the moral genius of the great American commoner....Men and measures must not claim him for their own. He remains the standard by which to measure men....Lincoln has become for us the test of human worth, and we honor men in the measure in which they approach the absolute standard of Abraham Lincoln. Other men may resemble and approach him; he remains the standard whereby all other men are measured and appraised...." Stephen S. Wise. (A President of World Jewish Congress)

"But though the world roars and rages about us, we must secure our peace of mind, a quiet place of tranquility and of order and of purpose within our own selves. For it is doubt and uncertainty of purpose and confusion of values which unnerves men. Peace of mind comes to men only when having faced all the issues clearly and without flinching, they have made their decision and are resolved......'You came into a great heritage made by the insight and the sweat and the blood of inspired and devoted and courageous men; thoughtlessly and in utmost self indulgence you have all but squandered this inheritance. Now only by the heroic virtues which made this inheritance can you restore it again.' It is written, 'You took the good things for granted. Now you must earn them again'. It is written, 'For every right that you cherish, you have a duty which you must fulfill. For every hope that you entertain, you have a task that you must perform. For every good that you wish to preserve, you will have to sacrifice your comfort and your ease. There is nothing for nothing any longer'......So here we are today. We are where we are because whenever we had a choice to make, we have chosen the alternative that required the least effort at the moment. There is organized mechanized evil loose in the world. But what has made possible its victories is the lazy, self-indulgent materialism, the amiable, lackadaisical, footless, confused complacency of the free nations of the world. They have dissipated, like wastrels and drunkards, the inheritance of freedom and order that came to them from hardworking, thrifty, faithful, believing and brave men. The disaster in the midst of which we are living is a disaster in the character of men. It is a catastrophe of the soul, of a whole generation which had forgotten, had lost, and had renounced the imperative and indispensable virtues of laborious, heroic, and honorable men." Walter Lippman. (American reporter, political commentator)

"We see and cherish diversity of ways, diversity of thoughts, of motives, and accomplishments. We don't seek to live anyone's life for him. We only seek to secure his rights, guarantee him opportunity to survive, with government performing only those needed and constitutionally sanctioned tasks which cannot otherwise be performed....for we Republicans define government's role where needed at many, many levels—preferably, though the one closest to the people involved; our towns and our cities, then our counties, then our states, then our regional contracts and only then the national government." Barry Goldwater (American Senator)

"We have built rockets and spaceships and shuttles; we have harnessed the atom, we have dazzled a generation with a display of our technological skills. But we still spend millions of dollars on aspirin and psychiatrists and tissues to wipe away the tears of anguish and uncertainty that result from our confusion and our emptiness....The closed circle of pure materialism is clear to us now—aspirations become wants, wants become needs, and self-gratification becomes a bottomless pit. All around us we have seen success in this world's terms become ultimate and desperate failures. Teenager and college students, raised in affluent surroundings and given all the material comforts our society can offer, commit suicide. Entertainer and sports figures achieve fame and wealth but find the world empty and dull without the solace of stimulation of drugs. Men and women rise to the top of their professions after years of struggling. But despite their apparent success, they are driven nearly mad by a frantic search for diversions, new mates, games, new experiences—anything to fill the diminishing interval between their existence and eternity--the way to serve yourself is to serve others; and that Aristotle was right, before them, when he said the only way to assure yourself happiness is to learn to give happiness." Mario Cuomo. (U.S. Governor)

"Success has made failures of many men." Cindy Adams (American gossip columnist and writer)

"A tomb now suffices him for whom the whole world was not sufficient." Unknown

"The rich have a passion for bargains as lively as it is pointless." Francoise Sagan (French playwright and novelist)

"He does not possess wealth; it possesses him." Benjamin Franklin (American author, printer, politician, scientist)

Chapter 4

Why is contentment selected as the goal for a meaningful life? The ultimate goal of life, it would seem, has to be something which is not a means to something else. One seeks wealth because it is viewed as leading to happiness or contentment; one seeks power, titles, winning contests, etc. all because they are seen as necessary to gain something else. You may ask why someone wants to be wealthy and they will give you an answer. If you ask someone why they want to be contented they would consider it a foolish question. You don't seek contentment to achieve something else. **IT IS THE END POINT**.

I have been around my share of people seeped in wealth or power or social status or fame, etc. enough to have understood how little contentment exists in their lives. No one denies we need a certain amount of wealth, health, social importance, freedom, power, etc. to maximize contentment. This is a no brainer. Not really of course, because many people manage, in their minds, to dismiss the less fortunate as having enough 'contentment' with their simple lives, and therefore need no help. You know, the slaves had their own simpletonian pleasures in life, as do the poor in our ghettoes, refugee camps, etc. And the wealthy owners would defend themselves by saying, "Without me, the slaves would perish. I feed them and shelter them and care for them when they are sick." Of course the average survival rate of slaves brought over was six years after landing. In modern times, at the very least all these less fortunates become irrelevant, 'gated off' from us—except maybe as a fetus needing protection from abortion. After birth all such concern evaporates. What a weird sense of ethics.

It was conceded earlier that humans need a certain amount of wealth, health, importance, freedom, and power to maximize contentment in their lives. The laws of evolution do not, however, create a level playing field for everyone. Unless one chooses to believe God Himself directs a certain sperm to combine with a certain egg, our birth was governed by chance. Unless one believes God personally involves Himself with us as individuals, annulling His own laws of evolution to aid us during our lives (of course only, or mostly, if we have inherited the right religious dogma), then we are on our own. EXCEPT, we really are not. Humans have an inherent sense of ethics which serves to put upon all of us a responsibility to help make a more level playing field for all. That is to say, we really can, collectively, enable the less fortunate to have more wealth and better health, provide them with a feeling of importance, afford them individual freedoms, and give them more power to control their own lives and destiny. While this is a collective responsibility, we cannot escape our individual responsibility to this collective effort without reducing our own chances for personal contentment.

This human inherent sense of ethics has two components. **OUR REASONING POWER MOLDS OUR ETHICAL PRINCIPLES**. And thus it is, that the Golden Rule is a universally accepted ethical principle. No one, to my knowledge, argues against the validity of the Golden Rule. What we do, in varying degrees is just conveniently ignore it when this rule clashes with other priorities in our life. We arrive at endorsing the Golden Rule via our ability to reason. We understand fairness. We simply understand it is not right that some should be landless, homeless, or live in refugee camps. We understand that it is not right for some children to receive poor childhood education. We understand that it is not right for some people to have poor health care. Clearly, if none of these things is not wrong, then nothing is wrong. Otherwise, it is every person for him/her self, just like in the lower species of the animal kingdom. A sense of ethics carries with it a sense of guilt. A sense of guilt prevents contentment. One can selfishly, using innate skills, amass wealth, good health, titles, power, and freedom for oneself BUT, no real sense of contentment will ever be achieved. There will be this puzzled head-scratching, and a feeling that 'I have so much, and yet I don't seem to be all that contented in life'. Not only that, but many of our acquisitions in life are age-related. One may have been a good athlete, but age will end that; one might have had good health, but age will change that; one might have had high titles, but age will see them fall by the way; one might have amassed vast material wealth, but the pleasures from that will have long-since faded; one might have been best friends with certain people, but time brings changes in everyone so that often the same two people no longer mesh together in the same way—the friendship is not the same. **CHANGE IS THE OPERATIVE WORD IN OUR LIVES**.

(6) Related Attestations:

"To be able to practice five things everywhere under heaven constitutes perfect virtue...gravity, generosity of soul, sincerity, earnestness, and kindness." Confucius

"We hold these truths to be self evident: that all men are created equal; that they are endowed by their Creator with certain unalienable rights; that among these are life, liberty, and the pursuit of happiness." Thomas Jefferson (American President)

"From each according to his abilities, to each according to his needs." Karl Marx (German philosopher)

"Those who deny freedom to others, deserve it not for themselves." Abraham Lincoln (American President)

"Ships that pass in the night, and speak each other in passing:
Only a signal shown and a distant voice in the darkness:
So on the oceans of life we pass and speak one another,
Only a look and a voice; then darkness again and a silence."
Henry Wadsworth Longfellow (U.S.poet)

"Three passions, simple but overwhelmingly strong, have governed my life; the longing for love, the search for knowledge, and unbearable pity for the suffering of mankind." Bertrand Russell (British philosopher)

"One of the worst things about life is not how nasty the nasty people are. You know that already. It is how nasty the nice people can be." Anthony Powell (British novelist)

"Men, their rights and nothing more; women, their rights and nothing less. Susan Anthony (American women's suffrage advocate)

"There are nine requisites for contented living: Health enough to make work a pleasure; Wealth enough to support your needs; Strength enough to battle with difficulties and forsake them; Grace enough to confess your sins and overcome them; Patience enough to toil until some good is accomplished; Charity enough to see some good in your neighbor; Love enough to make you useful and helpful to others; Faith enough to make real the things of God; Hope enough to remove all anxious fears concerning the future." Johann Wolfgang Von Goethe (German poet, dramatist, philosopher)

"A man's character is his fate." Heraclitus (Greek philosopher)

"What is hateful to thyself do not do to another. This is the whole Law, the rest is commentary." Hillel (Jewish rabbi, teacher)

"Where love rules, there is no will to power; and where power predominates, there love is lacking. The one is the shadow of the other." Carl Gustav Jung (Swiss psychologist, psychiatrist)

"In political speculations 'the tyranny of the majority' is not generally included among the evils against which society requires to be on its guard." John Stuart Mill (English political economist, philosopher)

"The love of glory, the fear of disgrace, the incentive to succeed, the desire to live in comfort, and the instinct to humiliate others are often the cause of that courage so renowned among men." Francois De La Rochefoucauld

"Race hatred is the cheapest and basest of all national passions, and it is the nature of hatred, as it is the nature of love, to change us into the likeness of that which we contemplate. We grow nobly like what we adore, and ignobly like what we hate....All hatreds, long persisted, bring us to every baseness for which we hated others." George Russell (Irish Poet, artist, essayist)

"We have just enough religion to make us hate, but not enough to make us love one another." Jonathan Swift (Irish satirist)

"I beg of you to remember that wherever our life touches yours we help or hinder—wherever your life touches ours, you make us stronger or weaker.... There is no escape—man drags man down, or man lifts man up." Booker T. Washington (American author, educator, and orator.)

"You can't go back home to your family—
to a young man's dream of fame and glory
to the country cottage away from strife and conflict
to the father you have lost
to the old forms and systems of things which seemed everlasting but are changing at the time."
Thomas Wolfe (American novelist)

"It is better to give than to lend, and it costs about the same." Sir Philip Gibbs (English journalist and novelist)

"Between the great things that we cannot do and the small things we will not do the danger is that we shall do nothing." Adolphe Monod (French Protestant Churchman)

"What do we live for, if it is not to make life less difficult to each other?" George Eliot (English novelist)

"There is so much good in the worst of us,
And so much bad in the best of us,
That it hardly behooves any of us
To talk about the rest of us". Edward Hoch (American writer)

"Hard to dislike a chap who likes you, isn't it? Well, there's your peace plan." Unknown

"Distrust all in whom the impulse to punish is powerful." Nietzsche (German philosopher, poet)

"Be not simply good, be good for something." Henry David Thoreau (American author and naturalist)

"I expect to pass through this world but once; any good thing therefore that I can do, or any kindness that I can show to any fellow creature, let me do it now; let me not defer or neglect it, for I shall not pass this way again." Stephen Grellet (French Quaker missionary)

"God, give us the serenity to accept the things that cannot be changed, the courage to change the things that can be changed, and the wisdom to know the difference." Reinhold Niebuhr (American theologian)

"Only when the last tree had died
And the last river been poisoned
And the last fish been caught
Will we realize that we cannot eat money." Cree Indian saying

"I shall show my faith by my works." Theodore Roosevelt (American President)

"The lives of the rich vary from rotten frivolity to rotten vice." Theodore Roosevelt (American President)

"Treat everybody with politeness, even those who are rude to you. You show courtesy to others not because they are gentlemen, but because you are." Unknown

"There are many persons of whom it may be said that they have no other possession in the world but their character, and yet they stand as firmly upon it as any crowned king." Samuel Smiles (Scottish author)

"The test of courage comes when we are in the minority; the test of tolerance comes when we are in the majority." Ralph W. Sockman (Church of Christ Minister)

"The three hardest tasks in the world are neither physical feats nor intellectual achievements, but moral acts; To return love for hate, to include the excluded, and to say, 'I was wrong'." Sydney Harris (essayist and drama Critic)

"A good person loves people and uses things, while a bad person loves things and uses people." Sydney Harris (Essayist and Drama Critic)

"Those who bring sunshine to the lives of others cannot keep it from themselves." James Matthew
Barrie (Scottish author and dramatist)

"Do all the good you can,
In all the ways you can,
In all the places you can,
At all the times you can,
To all the people you can
As long as ever you can." John Wesley (Church of England cleric and Christian theologian)

"Happiness is the only good
The place to be happy is here.
The time to be happy is now.

The way to be happy is to make others so." Robert G. Ingersoll (Civil War Veteran, political leader and orator)

"In my humble opinion, non-cooperation with evil is a much a duty as is cooperation with good. But in the past, non-cooperation has been deliberately expressed in violence to the evildoer. I am endeavoring to show to my countrymen that violent non-cooperation only multiplies evil and that as evil can only be sustained by violence, withdrawal of support of evil requires complete abstention from violence." Mohandas K. Gandhi (India Revolutionary leader)

"Care is not weakness. Care to us is the very essence, the greatest demonstration of strength. That's what makes us democratic socialists. That's what makes us so categorically different from them. We believe that strength without care is savage, and brutal, and selfish. It's the strength of the jungle. We believe that strength, with care, is compassion; the practical action that is needed to help people lift themselves to their full stature, their full potential. The strength to care. Not the strength of the jungle but the strength of humanity." Neil Kinnock. (Welsh politician)

"The most certain test by which we judge whether a country is really free is the amount of security enjoyed by minorities." Dean Acheson (United States Secretary of State)

"Civilization is a method of living, an attitude of equal respect for all men." Jane Addams (Founder of Hull House in Chicago, sociologist)

"Poverty is a bitter thing; but it is not as bitter as the existence of restless vacuity and physical, moral, and intellectual flabbiness, to which those doom themselves who elect to spend all their years in that vainest of all vain pursuits—the pursuit of mere pleasure as a sufficient end in itself." Teddy Roosevelt. (American President)

"The welfare of each of us is dependent fundamentally upon the welfare of all of us, and therefore in public life that man is the best representative of each of us who seeks to do good to each by doing good to all; in other words, whose endeavor it is not to represent any special class and promote merely that class's selfish interests, but to represent all true and honest men of all sections and all classes and work for their interests by working for our common country." Teddy Roosevelt. (American President)

"We keep countless men from being good citizens by the conditions of life with which we surround them." Teddy Roosevelt (American President)

Chapter 5

Let's pause here. Life, I contend in this musing, is by chance--and once life is started, every such life, in every species, is controlled by the God-created laws of evolution. We may want to be God's 'special edition' species, and each of us, if we play our cards right, wish to be favored by, and placed under the protection of God—BUT this is not a conclusion that can be arrived at via any kind of logical reasoning. Whether God EVER intervenes is beyond human insight. The evidence seems to be that, if so, rarely does He intervene. The road to contentment is via reason and ethics, uniquely developed characteristics of humans. The purpose of reason and ethics seems precisely to be the avenue that can lead to contentment. For reason or ethics to be developed and manifested effectively, then emotions need to be kept in check. Emotions like anger, jealousy, blind faith, hate, etc. are not helpful, but interfere with both reason and ethical behavior.

Reason, I reckon, **DEPENDS ON THE ACCUMULATION OF KNOWLEDGE**. People who spend most of their time being amused or working at mundane tasks, do not accumulate much knowledge. You can watch mindless type TV shows most of the day, and at the end of the day, your knowledge base has not grown. Good decisions cannot be made without knowledge. Humans, whose reasoning ability requires the accumulation of knowledge, require a long formative stage of life. Humans are not exactly born, and then a few hours later, up and running fast enough to escape most predators. In fact we humans are our own worst predators. Both reason and ethics take years of practice and thinking—**ABSENT INTERFERENCE FROM EXCESSIVE EMOTIONS**—before any kind of substantial contentment can be achieved.

ETHICS IS NOT SLOPPY SORRINESS. It is of little use to say, "Turn off the TV, I can't stand watching these poor wretches in a refugee camp," etc. There are people who spend a good amount of time verbally expressing their compassion for the poor and the less fortunate of all sorts. Their words drip with compassion. Then they go about their way piling up more wealth than they really need, supporting the politics which favor the rich and prey on the poor and less fortunate. But everything is ok—they may go to church every Sunday and put some nominal amount of money in a plate, the vast percentage of which will simply go to salaries, building expenses, etc. All of this is useless compassion, and **IT IS NOT ETHICS**. Ethics involves both the ability to understand the problem and THEN commit to personally doing something about it. Again, ETHICS IS NOT SLOPPY SORRINESS. Ethics is not just understanding right from wrong—**it is acting to do the right**. We have a whole lifetime to get it right. How many ever get it right would be pure speculation, as is how many, to what extent, ever end up contented in life.

Each of us has our place in the cosmos, but we can only be content with our place if we recognize our significance to the whole. Egocentric notions, no matter how much we desire a more important personal role in the cosmos, serve as no help in achieving contentedness. The more we attach ourselves to the illusion of our own self importance, the less likely we are to go with the evolutionary flow, so to speak, and the more likely we are to feel frustrated, stressed, and betrayed by religious dogmas which lead us to believe we really can be 'special'— that the laws of evolution don't apply to us. There is no clear evidence that Divine intervention is available to us as individuals, as a particular group, or as a particular nation. The reality is, that to the Universe, of which we are a part, **WE ARE ALL DISPENSABLE.** No rational person eagerly joins in to play a poker game and then becomes infuriated when the dealer won't slip them cards under the table, especially after giving him some money, praising him effusively, and building a glittering temple in his honor. Refusal to accept this individual dispensabililty blocks our efforts to be contented. The best of people die, the most beloved of pets die—no pocket of life is indispensable.

In judging good from bad we need keep this in perspective: **THE COLLECTIVE GOOD, FOR THE GREATEST NUMBER, IS ALWAYS BETTER THAN THE GOOD FOR ANY INDIVIDUAL, ANY FAMILY, ANY SECT, ANY COMMUNITY, ANY NATION.** "Family values" is not an admirable state, but a highly selfish state in which the measure of things is based on the benefit to a particular 'family'. Herein lies the strength of moral character: to do the good thing, to do the right thing for the good of the greatest number of people, to help level the playing field for the less fortunate, to meet the basic needs of all humanity—all of this requires the moral strength to act in the interest of the greatest good to the less fortunate. We may have our own special family, friends, group, or nation, BUT God's family is the entire spectrum of His created universe. When people inform me they have been 'saved' it strikes me as the ultimate self serving declaration.

Some of these same people meet with horrible tragedies in their lives. It just doesn't jive, or God has been jiving with them. If you aren't in the game you can't win anything. So being in the game of life, by chance, gives all of us the chance to have a meaningful life, which, as defined here, means attaining a high degree of contentment with our lives—a self-developed, society-aided earned contentment.

The role of friendship to contentment is tricky. If we follow the Golden Rule we will have friends, if by friends we mean people who will help us when in need. Then there are friends with whom we mesh well personality-wise. These are people with whom we enjoy the other's company and doing things together. **HOWEVER**, people change with time, distance may intervene, relevance in daily lives may change, and this makes many good friendships of limited duration. When good friendships fade away for factors which include passage of time, changed personalities, and physical distance, there is no tragedy. The memories which remain are definitely valuable for contentment. And of course there are friends of the moment, people who become part of your daily interactions, who are useful, and necessary to your current life. They come and go like ships in the night. Friendships are important to anyone's life, especially the good memories, BUT one need be careful in thinking good friends alone can bring contentment. No one is really content if they are dependent on others to control or run their lives. This is a dangerous game. Others die, move away, experience personality changes, have a change in their health status or in their lives in such ways as to leave us on our own. Many elderly are unhappy because so many of their friends are gone. They were so dependent on certain others to enrich their lives that life without these others is unpleasant. In the best of marriages, for example, one usually dies a good time before the other, while many marriages don't last, or are reduced to feigned tolerance. Children grow up and leave the nest, and if they don't, that often indicates a family values, circle-the-wagons, walled-off, growth-stilted existence. Whenever we find ourselves circling wagons and shutting out others as irrelevant to our lives, this does not bode well for our own contentment. The entire process of evolution is built around diversity, not stagnant sameness. To reject diversity as an intriguing and positive aspect of life is to spend our lives swimming upstream against the very living process into which we were born.

(7) Relevant Attestations:

"God gave us memories so that we might have roses in December." J.M. Barrie (Scottish author and dramatist)

"Laugh a little more at your own troubles and a little less at your neighbor's." Unknown

"City life: millions of people being lonesome together." Henry David Thoreau (American author and naturalist)

"Bring me all your flowers now
I would rather have a single rose
From the garden of a friend
Than have the choicest flowers,
When my stay on Earth must end.
I would rather have the kindest words
Which may now be said to me,
Than flattered when my heart is still—
And this life has ceased to be.
I would rather have a loving smile
From the friends I know are true,

Than tears shed round my casket,
When this world I've bade adieu!
Bring me all your flowers,
Whether pink, or white or red.
I'd rather have one blossom now
Than a truckload when I'm dead." R. D. Richards (poet)

Chapter 6

We all know people who have been against almost all the changes in society which expanded freedom to others, expanded justice to others, expanded wealth to others, etc. These people are never happy campers, whose thought processes include the oft repeated phrase "I can't stand..........". And if you can't stand all sorts of others you cannot be contented. There is one person from whom you cannot get away, and that is yourself. Therefore, one should never be more contented than when being alone, at or away from home, doing things often that you like, by yourself, as a special treat to enjoy your own self, in your own way, on your own time, with few distractions to interfere with the tranquility you should find there. If we cannot be tranquil and contented in moments by ourselves, then contentment will not be achieved in the presence of others either. We all need to understand ourselves as well as appreciate the diversity of others if we are to achieve contentment. Since reasoned behavior is a component necessary for the achievement of contentment, we must be able to detach ourselves from our immediate surroundings in order to free our minds for thoughtful action. It is hard to have deep thoughts if most of your time is spent babbling with others over inconsequential matters via modern technological devices. Endless mindless communication over trivial crap is hardly conducive to any sort of in-depth quality reasoning over matters like the meaning of life.

(8) Relevant Attestations:

"We now communicate with everyone, and say absolutely nothing. We have reconstructed the Tower of Babel. and it is a television's antenna (and lots of other gadgets). A thousand voices producing a daily parody of democracy, in which everyone's opinion is afforded equal weight, regardless of substance or merit. Indeed, it can even be argued that opinions of real weight tend to sink with barely a trace in television's ocean of banalities." Ted Koppel (American broadcast journalist)

"Voluntary loneliness, isolation from others, is the readiest safeguard against the unhappiness that may arise out of human relations." Sigmund Freud (Austrian psychologist)

"I have never found the companion that was so companionable as solitude." Henry David Thoreau (American libertarian writer)

"I think I could turn and live with animals, they are so placid and self-contained....
They do not lie awake in the dark and weep for their sins,
They do not make me sick discussing their duty to God,
Not one is dissatisfied, not one is demented with the mania of owning things, not one kneels to another,
Nor to his kind that lived thousands of years ago,
Not one is respectable or unhappy over the whole earth." Walt Whitman (American poet)

"After a while you learn the subtle difference
Between holding a hand and chaining a soul,
And you learn that love doesn't mean leaning
And company doesn't mean security,
And you begin to learn that kisses aren't contracts
And presents aren't promises,
And you begin to accept your defeats
With your head up and your eyes open,
With the grace of an adult, not the grief of a child,
And learn to build all your roads
On today because tomorrow's ground
Is too uncertain for plans, and futures have
A way of falling down in mid-flight.
After a while you learn that even sunshine
Burns if you get too much.
So you plant your own garden and decorate
Your own soul, instead of waiting
For someone to bring you flowers.
And you learn that you really can endure...
That you really are strong
And you really do have worth.
And you learn and learn....
With every goodbye you learn." Unknown

"Millions long for immortality who don't know what to do with themselves on a rainy Sunday afternoon." Susan Ertz. (British Fiction Writer and novelist)

"By all means sometimes be alone: salute thyself: see what thy soul doth wear: dare to look in thy chest, and tumble up and down what thou findest there." W. Wordsworth (English Poet)

"We're all in this alone." Lily Tomlin (American actress, comedienne)

"The man who follows the crowd will usually get no further than the crowd. The man who walks alone is likely to find himself in places no one has ever been before. Creativity in living is not without its attendant difficulties, for peculiarity breeds contempt. And the unfortunate thing about being ahead of your time is that when people finally realize you were right, they'll say it was obvious all along. You have two choices in life: you can dissolve into the mainstream, or you can be distinct. To be distinct, you must be different. To be different, you must strive to be what no one else but you can be." Alan Ashley-Pitt. (Western Film)

Chapter 7

If we are going to find meaning in our lives we are going to have to find it in a world that is imperfect and unfair. This is the reality. But the point should not be lost that humans have the inherent ability to make the world more perfect and more fair for those humans less fortunate for any of many reasons. The Pope can pray for peace like clockwork every New Year's Eve but it is simply ludicrous, and any reasonable person knows it. If it has **NEVER** worked in the past why will it ever work? And if we can find a rare instance when wars ended shortly after New Year the question begs why does this work only once in a while? No, it is more evident that we have met the enemy and it is us. People don't have to be hungry, people don't have to be left without medical care, kids don't have to be left in poor schools for education, people don't have to deny privileges to certain others--because we all, collectively, have the ability to end almost all of this. God's laws of evolution have evolved to the point where we collectively have the ability to help the less fortunate— so why then is it God's responsibility, through our prayers, to do what we collectively can do ourselves?

Of course, once born, this is a bad omen for the likelihood of death. One can pray not to die, but why would anyone have the self-serving audacity to suggest God should prevent anyone from dying? Evolution simply doesn't work that way, and the evolutionary process **IS NOT ABOUT** individual members of any species at any specific time in this process. When any of us starts thinking this process can be bent to meet our own individual needs we need to come to grips with reality. Once we never were, and soon we will never be again. There was no pain in not existing before, and there is no logical reason to feel there will be any pain when we don't exist again. What exactly is our gripe? If we can't handle existing we can decease ourselves. I doubt God will be upset at all. I sometimes wonder who was the idiot who came up with the notion— labeled faith-based fact—that God will decide when someone's time is up, and no one else? How silly can we get? If someone mugs me and shoots me dead in the process, this is God's directive? I can't believe at all in a God who is emotionally unbalanced and vindictive, some kind of evil Godfather. Life is not meaningless, it just is never about us as individuals. If we believe otherwise, real contentment will be out of reach.

(9) Relevant Attestations:

"We are always making God our accomplice, so that we may legalize our iniquities. Every successful massacre is consecrated by a Te Deum, and the clergy have never been wanting in benedictions for any victorious enormity." Henri Frederic Amiel (Swiss philosopher)

"I now pray to God that he will bless in the years to come our work, our deeds, our foresight, our resolve; that the almighty may protect us from both arrogance and cowardly servility, that he may help us find the right way which he has laid down for the

German people and that he may always give us courage to do the right thing and never to falter or weaken before any power or any danger. Long live Germany and the German people." Adolf Hitler. (German dictator)

"Serving God is doing Good to Man, but praying is thought an easier service, and therefore more generally chosen." Benjamin Franklin (American author, printer, political theorist, politician, postmaster, scientist, musician, inventor)

Chapter 8

Emotions play a big role in our lives, but **REASONABLE MORAL DECISIONS ARE BEST MADE WHEN OUR EMOTIONS ARE UNDER CONTROL**. If I don't like the way somebody dresses, for example, that emotion is not a legitimate reason for in any way interfering with their choice of dress. Maybe sexually explicit dress is the exception, covered by the Golden Rule. All of these emotional irrational feelings can be controlled and reason employed to do away with them. It is really a no brainer. If somebody doesn't like the way I dress I would not like them empowered with the right to tell me how to dress. And I, in return, will not tell them how they can dress. If I don't like the way they dress then I will be sure not to dress that way myself. Music, food, sex, sports, art, religious beliefs, etc. are all personal variations. **THAT IS THE WAY EVOLUTION WORKS**. Don' worry about it, in the end everything gets ironed out even if it takes a million years.

(10) Relevant Attestations:

"The man who gets angry at the right things and with the right people, and in the right way and at the right time and for the right length of time, is commended." Aristotle. (Greek philosopher)

"He that would govern others, first should be the master of himself." Philip Massinger (English dramatist)

"Sincerity is all that counts. It's a wide-spread modern heresy. Think again. Bolsheviks are sincere. Facists are sincere. Lunatics are sincere. People who believe the earth is flat are sincere. They can't all be right. Better make certain first you've got something to be sincere about and with." Tom Driberg (British politician, journalist and author)

"Some of the worst men in the world are sincere and the more sincere they are the worse they are." Lord Hailsham (British politician)

"The less men reason, the more wicked they are. Savages, princes, nobles, and dregs of the people, are commonly the worst of men, because they reason least." Paul Henri Thiry, Baron D'holbach (French materialist, philosopher)

"All men who deliberate on controversial matters, should be free from hate, friendship, anger and pity." Sallust (Roman historian)

"Consider how much more you often suffer from your anger and grief, than from those very things for which you are angry and grieved." Marcus Aurelius Antoninus (Roman Emperor)

"The command of one's self is the greatest empire a man can aspire unto, and consequently, to be subject to our own passions is the most grievous slavery. He who best governs himself is best fitted to govern others." John Milton (English poet)

"Like an unchecked cancer, hate corrodes the personality and eats away its vital unity. Hate destroys a man's sense of values and his objectivity. It causes him to describe the beautiful as ugly and the ugly as beautiful, and to confuse the true with the false and the false with the true. Darkness cannot drive out darkness; only light can do that. Hate cannot drive out hate; only love can do that. Hate multiplies hate, violence multiplies violence, and toughness multiplies toughness in a descending spiral of destruction....The chain reaction of evil—hate begetting hate, wars producing more wars—must be broken, or we shall be plunged into the dark abyss of annihilation." Martin Luther King (American civil rights leader)

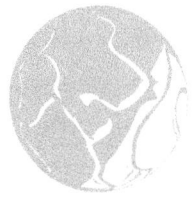

Chapter 9

M**AJORITY RULE CANNOT BE USED TO MEASURE RIGHT AND WRONG.** "If you don't like it here you can leave" is about the most ignorant way possible to decipher right from wrong. "I can't stand....." is no way of proving anything regarding the substance of any issue. "I believe....." is a self-admission that whatever comes next is not fact. The basis for virtue is always reason. "Do unto others as you would have them do unto you, were you in their shoes" is a universal ethical principle precisely because it is a reasoned ethical principle. How would we argue against this being a moral principle? A person hardly has to go to college and major in religion or to inherit the right religion to understand ethics. The most common commoner who practices the Golden Rule can be as ethical as the most titled priest dressed in the finest garb, speaking from the pulpit of the most ornate church, from the thickest holy book, in the most erudite words. We need cut to the chase and stop pretending ethics is complicated. The only thing that complicates ethics is when we tie ourselves into a pretzel trying to justify why we are not following the Golden Rule. Interestingly, all these justifications are always self-serving. We all fail to varying degrees. We, for example, could refuse to buy any product made by 'slave labor' (those earning non-living wages), BUT our doing this would put no dent in the practice at all. Besides, we like bargains, and the more things we buy at bargain prices the more things we can buy, and the more things we can buy the happier we will be. This notion is all a lie, a tragic lie, but it serves our own selfish emotional needs.

According to Buddha a good deal of life is suffering. **SUFFERING IS THE PRICE OF EVOLUTIONARY GAIN**. No pain, no gain. This human suffering is caused by our inability to recognize that things are impermanent, selfless, and interdependent. We need to understand that **EVERYTHING CHANGES**, that life on this planet is not about individuals, that everything around us is interdependent. It is this interdependency and change which are the centerpiece brilliancy of the evolutionary process—not individual 'salvation', 'redemption', 'assistance', 'protection', or divine 'intervention'. We may, as individuals, wish to be the center of Divine attention and protection, but it has no basis in reason. I cannot think of any solid reason why anyone on earth has been given a raw deal. It would be like someone in a poker game blaming the dealer for his/her bad cards, and becoming angry if the dealer would not slip him/her better cards under the table, especially if he/she had gone to great pains to praise and fawn over the dealer on a daily basis. I mean, what has he/she done wrong? He/she made the dealer an item of 'worship', an object of fawning respect, and then the dealer doesn't slip him/her needed cards under the table! Sure the dealer could stack the deck or slip him/her cards during the game, but he doesn't. It seems evident that those who wait on God to slip them some cards under the table are chasing up the wrong tree. God created a system where we had a remote chance to exist—and here we are—we do exist, and we have the innate potential to achieve some contentment—and the more people who follow the Golden

Rule the more people who will end up with some contentment. So what is our bitch really?

And so it goes with the Creator of the evolutionary process. If we want to be in the game, we play the cards we get the best we can. No one has any gun to our heads demanding we have to stay in the game. We have the power to end our lives if, at some point, we have had enough. **A CONTENTED PERSON ACCEPTS THE ROLES OF CHANCE, DIVERSITY, AND DIFFERING ENVIRONMENTS IN LIFE**. To a large extent many of our environmental factors are incidental to contentedness. Many people who have acquired a great amount of material wealth ponder why they are not happier than in younger days before all the wealth. Wealth does not create contentedness, power does not create contentedness, personal attractiveness does not create contentedness, sexual excess does not create contentedness, fame does not create personal contentedness, popularity for the wrong reasons does not create contentedness, believing in life after death does not create contentedness. Rather, **MAXIMIZING THE USE OF REASON AND PRACTICED ETHICS IS THE PATHWAY TO CONTENTEDNESS HERE ON EARTH**.

Understanding the 'nature' of life is essential to any 'meaningful life'. **IF WE CANNOT COMPREHEND UNFAIRNESS, A NON-LEVEL PLAYING FIELD, AND OUR OWN PLACE IN THE PROCESS OF EVOLUTION, AND THEN PROPERLY MIX ALL THIS WITH OUR OWN PECULIAR PERSONALITY, TALENTS, AND PHYSICAL STATUS, THEN CONTENTMENT IN LIFE IS OUT OF REACH**. Those who adopt a faith-based belief in religious dogma—inherited, not reasoned out—are destined all their lives to be disappointed, forced to lamely dismiss all personal tragedy in life as 'God's mysterious ways'. The worst of everything is explained away as having some purpose beyond our understanding. This of course is a sham to one's comprehension ability. It is a sham because, mumble all of this unfairness away as we might, there still always remains the question "Why Me?", "Why them?", "What am I doing wrong", etc. Trapped into a mindless faith based worship of inherited religious dogma, there is no apparent way out except to pray harder, more often; to go through more rituals more often; to put a little more money in the collection plate; to be selectively kinder to those in a position to further your own interests, etc. Mindless desperation and a self-centered 'family values' mind-set just leads one to a life of feeling besieged, frustrated, inadequate, and powerless. Well, at least heaven is just around the corner—**EXCEPT**, none of us know that for sure. It is like Santa Claus is still there—we just have to be better children to get some better gifts in life. This is not reasoned belief; it is self-serving desperation. We need never be reduced to behaving like the mafia leader who attends church every Sunday. The only certainty is that he will not meet any of his dead victims at the service.

It is not possible to understand our role in life or how to have a meaningful life if we don't understand the basic laws which govern God's created process of evolution. **EVOLUTION ADVANCES BASED ON GENETIC VARIATION, ENVIRONMENTAL VARIATION, CHANCE, AND SURVIVAL OF THE FITTEST**. Diversity drives the whole process, which explains the uneven playing field. Individuals and environments vary because if they don't there is no way for evolutionary progress. WHAT WE PERCEIVE AS UNFAIRNESS IS REALLY DIVERSITY. Some people are genetically 'better' than others. Some environments are 'better' than others for survival of certain individuals. Unless we insist on making the assumption that the human species is the end product of evolution, there is little logic or reason to believe we are **GOD'S CHOSEN ANYTHING** let alone have been given 'dominion' over other species. We don't talk about God giving cats dominion over frogs or whatever, because that seems silly. **WE WANT BADLY TO BELIEVE GOD THINKS OF US INDIVIDUALLY JUST AS WE DO ABOUT OUR PETS.** With our pets we have a personal relationship. If we didn't benefit from this we wouldn't have pets. God, by definition, is all powerful, at least compared to us. Humans have special affinity to their own children—of course, they are the closest thing to a creation of our own. God's creation is the evolutionary process and all the varied species are His creations. When the expression 'all God's children' is used, the implication is to mean all of humanity. BUT this is logically irrational. After all, **ALL SPECIES, IN THIS ANALOGY, WOULD REPRESENT 'ALL GOD'S CHILDREN'.** The American Indians, with their reverence to animals and trees and natural resources, were not as silly as most of us would like to believe. We may tend to belittle all this 'sacred' this and 'sacred' that in Indian culture but a lot of this belittlement reflects our own self-anointed inflated importance in the evolutionary scheme.

Anyone who takes the Golden Rule seriously is ethically wounded by the current fate of so many humans on this planet. There is a reason for this ethical wound—**HUMANS DO HAVE THE POWER TO ELIMINATE SO MUCH OF THE SUFFERING.** In terms of sheer numbers, there are more humans suffering today than ever before in the history of humans on this planet. Humans are not only the direct cause of this current massive species extinction unfolding before our eyes, but **OUR FAILURE TO ENFORCE REPRODUCTIVE RESPONSIBILITY IS THE REASON WHY OUR IMPACT ON OTHER SPECIES AND ON OUR NATURAL RESOURCES IS RAPIDLY DESTROYING BOTH.** We cannot see the forest for the sake of the trees. And we don't understand relativity. Does anyone seriously believe most American Indians are more contented today than in the days of

Columbus? I have read books by the 'Lost Children' of Africa who saw their entire families murdered, tortured, and raped by others who wanted their land. Some of these children, by the thousands, aged 5 to teenagers, had to trek 2000 miles to reach the safety of refugee camps. A small number of survivors now live in places like the United States. When they write, they don't write about how contented they are in a modern industrialized society—no, they write about how much they miss the simple life they were living before all this tragedy happened. Their fondest memories are of a toy, or a blanket, or a pair of shorts, or playmates now dead. I enjoy all the conveniences of modern life, but I can't say there was no pleasure in my youth when I had so much less. And I also know that if I had, by chance, been born 100 years earlier I would have died a very young death. As a child I had every disease imaginable but there was medicine available to save me from dying. In a different age I would have just died. In earlier times you needed a bunch of offspring because most of them would die young. Today, most will live for a long time and this results in the current overpopulation crisis. More live, and more live longer. If humans, as a species, cannot understand population dynamics, and the **EFFECT OVERPOPULATION HAS ON** other species, the natural resources of our planet, and on the quality of human life for more and more people—if we cannot understand this—then no species is more innately suited to wage effective genocidal warfare amongst its own members. Terrorism is uniquely qualified to be the last method available to make dramatic population control happen. It won't be the first time in evolutionary history that a massive event occurs which reshuffles the evolutionary cards on the table for the next hand.

The poignant point above is this: one cannot proceed with achieving personal contentment if one is oblivious to the precarious global state of humanity in this present day. **TUNNEL VISION IMPLIES**

ALL THAT MATTERS IS THE SIZE OF THE PIE, RIGHT NOW TODAY, FOR ONESELF OR ONE'S IMMEDIATE FAMILY. If this is the entire picture from which one makes daily decisions, then one's entire comprehension of life is one of a self-serving rat race. **WHEN ONE'S LIFE BECOMES A RAT RACE, IN AND OF ITSELF, THERE IS NO POSSIBILITY OF PERSONAL CONTENTMENT**. Add to this mixture a strong dose of faith based salvation acquired through inherited religion, and the genocidal mentality is heavily armed. The strongest motivation to behave unethically—that is, against the Golden Rule—is via a belief that God Himself endorses emotional behavior designed to meet selfish ends. It is always easy to kill someone, deprive them of rights, of wealth, of medical care, of a good education, of a level playing field **IF GOD SO WISHES YOU TO DO SO**. And this is true whether it be one individual, whole ethnic/religious groups, or a whole nation. The worst unethical atrocities are achieved when bugles are blaring and people in large numbers attack others via a God-endorsed common attack. Eerily, we no longer need bugles and huge armies, just sufficient anger, the right amount of religious faith in some inherited religion, or perceived best form of government, or best ethnicity—plus access to others via gadget communication—and the means to create havoc and destruction are at hand. If we really think acts of terrorism can be prevented we are suffering just one more illusion. The correlation between the human conditions behind these attacks is commensurate with the number of such attacks. Stated yet another way, with a world already overpopulated by humans, **EVERY FURTHER INCREASE IN OUR POPULATION ON THIS PLANET WILL MULTIPLY EXPONENTIALLY THE NUMBER OF DEATHS VIA TERRORISM**.

If we sufficiently fathom the nature of all the individual suffering imbedded in the evolutionary process, and we properly evaluate our own weaknesses and strengths, then we are in a position, then and only then, to achieve a contented life through reason and ethical behavior. **IN THE END, WE DO WHAT WE CAN, AS BEST WE CAN, FOR AS LONG AS WE CAN, NOT BECAUSE IT WILL BE A TICKET TO SOME UNKNOWABLE HEAVEN, BUT BECAUSE IT IS THE ONLY WAY TO ACHIEVE A CONTENTED LIFE—A SORT OF HEAVEN ON EARTH.** This is not to deny that for reasons of genetics or environment some simply cannot be contented in their lives. There is such a thing as real tragedy—hopeless tragedy—some of it imposed by genetics, some of it imposed by environment, and some of it controlled by luck. In the absence of human overpopulation, human rights have evolved in the right direction—a sort of social evolution to go along with the more obvious physical evolution. Through it all, the least happy campers, the least contented portion of human society, have been those who always resist the expansion of human rights to those without them. Their tenacious attachment to tradition and selected scriptural quotations from ages ago always places them on the wrong side of the battle, always necessitating these social advances having to be stuffed down their throats. These are the "if you don't like it here you can leave", the "I can't stand"ers, the "I don't want to talk about it" crowd, the war enthusiasts, the religious literalists—trapped in life with braces on their brains, almost always opposed to science as dictum over faith.

There is a term in Buddhism called 'karuna'. Karuna is often defined as compassion. But this is oversimplification. The Golden Rule obviously involves compassion. There is no way a person can follow the Golden Rule without compassion. But then, **WE CAN'T HAVE COMPASSION IF WE HAVE NO APPRECIATION OF DIVERSITY. WE CAN'T HAVE AN APPRECIATION OF DIVERSITY IF WE DO NOT UNDERSTAND THE BASIC LAWS OF EVOLUTION.** All of these things are very much interrelated.

And we CANNOT reach a state of contentment without adherence to the Golden Rule. The problem with religious fanatics is that they abandon the Golden Rule and become obsessed with a belief that God is very much involved with their personal lives and destiny. Their God is often some kind of strict, inflexible, sadist—Who punishes human infractions of His laws. HE, at least in part, does this via HIS chosen human followers, almost always chosen by means of inherited religious dogma. This kind of faith-based ethical value package has been around since the early years of human history. Only the particulars have differed. Whatever else may be gained from this kind of devotion, and certainly hope for life after death is one of the gains, these people never seem to be a very contented lot.

Karuna is not about some sort of vague feeling, best described as a sort of 'sloppy sympathy'. There are an abundant number of people dripping with sympathy, 'in theory', with the less fortunate. But, with these people, while their vague mushy feelings are trotted out as proof of their moral fiber, they practice their ethical state of mind through prayers, or via token contributions for someone else 'somewhere' to help these people, and maybe a rare personal involvement with someone less fortunate--most likely some blood relative. **FOR COMPASSION TO BE GENUINE ETHICS, THE KIND WHICH IS GOING TO LEAD TO PERSONAL CONTENTMENT, THE COMPASSION HAS TO BE OF AN ENGAGED NATURE.** Embedded in karuna are said to be the six perfections—generosity, propriety, patience, effort, meditation, and wisdom.

We need pause again. We learn to accept the nature of the world in which we live. We know everything is subject to change; that impermanence is everywhere we look; that we as individuals are not the center of anything; that God rarely, if ever, intervenes with His own laws which control the evolutionary process; that for us to begin to achieve contentment in our lives we must use human reason and our inherent sense of ethics to govern our lives. We are not 'special', we have no ability to remotely know anything about life after death, or any reasonable basis to believe such a thing exists; there is no basis to believe humans are the end species in the evolutionary process; rather, reason dictates humans have the innate ability to relieve the suffering of the less fortunate by direct interaction with them. We have an obligation to always support policies which level the playing field for the greatest number of people, and we understand human contentment is not always attainable for reasons of genetics and environmental variations, that it is each individual's right to control their own choices in life which do not act adversely on others, including their own dying process. We understand, through reason, that God is not determining which sperm connects with which egg at what period in time, and that God is not determining how and when an individual dies or should die. We have also learned to correctly analyze our own particular strengths and weaknesses. **WHEN ALL THIS IS FINALLY IN PLACE, THEN WE CAN BEGIN TO LIVE OUR LIVES IN SUCH A WAY AS TO MAXIMIZE CONTENTMENT IN OUR LIVES.** This goal is the meaning of life.

If personal contentment is the goal chosen to achieve a meaningful life, then the word, as used, must be defined. Contentment is not a word with a precise meaning. Nor would I contend the achievement of contentment is lacking in variation from person to person. The road to contentment as well as the level of contentment will vary dependent on the individual genetic and environmental circumstances. But contentment means, in this context, a life in which there is not an endless series of things to complain about, argue about; things needed above and beyond the basics; a need to constantly look over one's shoulder to see who is gaining; a need to constantly out-plan, out-maneuver, out-smart, or out-perform some one to gain title, power, or financial gain. **CONTENTMENT REFERS TO ONE'S PERSONAL LIFE, NOT WITH ANY SATISFACTION OR DISSATISFACTION REGARDING THE STATE OF THE WORLD, POLITICAL REALITIES, OR PREVAILING RELIGIOUS VIEWS.**

Contentment does not mean the world is just the way you want it, or your country is just the way you want it, or your job is just the way you want it, or you have everything you might want in life, or that your family and friends are all doing fine. For this to spoil your own contented state would imply you personally are responsible for these things. Of course none of us are. If we want to see great advances in the state of the world, or life kingdoms, come back again in a million years. Change is constant, great changes come about slowly or via massive sudden upheavals that have happened on occasion in evolutionary history.

But we must be careful here. If we personally cannot change ALL of what needs to be changed in this current state of life on earth, we can—**ALL OF US**—with excess on our plates—alleviate **SOME** of the injustices and misfortunes into which so many other humans and varied species are trapped today. That is the obligation thrust on us by our ethical nature. Ethics involves obligations. This is to say right and wrong imply, by definition, that there are certain obligatory actions required for ethical rewards to be achieved. It can, of course, be believed that ethical rewards come as a heaven for the righteous people after death. That possibility is simply unanswerable and past human powers of comprehension. **ANYONE, BELIEVING SOMETHING, DOES NOT MAKE IT SO.** Thus, this leaves reward for ethical behavior as something attained right here on earth. I have suggested contentment is the reward gained for using reason, and reasoned out ethics, in an active way as the road to such contentment.

The inherent ethical trait of human beings rejects, by the nature of the universal Golden Rule, any notion that others don't count or need not count. The current 'family values' way of thinking is almost antithetical to ethics. It is just another way of implying "I count", or 'we' count, while others don't". It is just that the 'I' has been expanded to include immediate genetic family. A parent obviously has the obligation to create a healthy environment for a child during the formative years of the child. But once a child passes from such an obligatory protective environment, this obligation vanishes, at least in terms of any ethical treatment of grown offspring versus any other adults in the world. The latter is a tricky statement. Of course a parent can have special feelings for their offspring forever. This is natural and admirable. Just like someone might be your friend forever, that is admirable too. BUT, there is no special ethical requirement that friendship must last, that marriage must last or, that there is an ethical obligation to treat grown offspring differently than others in terms of the Golden Rule. I suppose one could say parental responsibility is not forever in the absence of special circumstances, whereas ethical responsibility to others (including offspring) is forever. In a practical sense this means if you have excess resources past what is needed for basic living, these excess resources, according to the Golden Rule, need be shared with those having the greatest needs, not bestowed as gifts of any sort to those with no great needs, and this includes your own offspring. Nowhere in the teachings of the great prophets of any religion, or in the Golden Rule, is there any attempt to justify the accumulation of wealth by genetic connections. Nowhere. One may wish to put one's family first in case of sharing wealth, but this is to be found nowhere else in ethical cannon from either prophets or the Golden Rule. If I were an orphan in a refugee camp in need of food or shelter I would wish those, with excess to share, would share it with me before a relative with no such needs. And so would anyone else. Can anyone really imagine Christ encouraging us to leave our excess wealth, upon death, to affluent offspring rather than to those least fortunate in the world? Can anyone imagine Christ telling us that 'we earned our affluence, it is all ours to keep and spend on ourselves or other family members'? This would really be the ultimate stretch of distortion. Yet this is exactly what organized religion has done to ethical meaning–distorted it by filling up religious worship and behavior with all sorts of meaningless rituals, pablum- like sermons, etc. Most clergy are like politicians, they tell us what we want to hear lest we abandon their message and head elsewhere. While clergy do not tell us to give our excess wealth to our kids and not to the poor, they do not BUT—the silence is deafening and suffices to give us wiggle room.

(11) Relevant attestations:

"Our object in the construction of the state is the greatest happiness of the whole, and not that of any one class (or family)." Plato (Greek philosopher)

"Two nations; between whom there is no intercourse and no sympathy; who are as ignorant of each other's habits, thoughts, and feelings, as if they were dwellers in different zones, or inhabitants of different planets; who are formed by a different breeding, are fed by a different food, are ordered by different manners, and are not governed by the same laws. 'You speak of– ' said Egremont, hesitantly, 'THE RICH AND THE POOR'." Benjamin Disraeli (British statesman)

"He who begins by loving Christianity better than Truth will proceed by loving his own sect or church better than Christianity, and end by loving himself better than all. Samuel Taylor Coleridge (British poet)

"The majestic egalitarianism of the law, which forbids rich and poor alike to sleep under bridges, to beg in the streets, and to steal bread." Anatole France (French writer)

"I have had no real gratification or enjoyment of any sort more than my neighbor on the next block who is worth only a half million." William Henry Vanderbilt (U.S. railway chief)

"I am the poor white, fooled and pushed apart,
I am the Negro, bearing slavery's scar,
I am the Red man, driven from the land,
I am the immigrant clutching the hope I seek–
And finding only the same old stupid plan,
Of dog eat dog, or might crush the weak." Langston Hughes (American poet)

"The moral flabbiness born of the exclusive worship of the bitch-goddess SUCCESS. That—with the squalid cash interpretation put on the word "success"—is our national disease." William James (American psychologist, philosopher)

"No nation can last, which has made a mob of itself, however generous at heart. It must discipline it's passions, and direct them or they will discipline it, one day, with scorpion-whips. Above all, a nation cannot last in a money-making job; it cannot with impunity,–it cannot with existence—go on despising literature, despising science, despising nature, despising compassion, and concentrating its soul on Pence." John Ruskin (British writer).

"In this world it is not what we take up, but what we give up, that makes us rich." H.W. Beecher (American clergyman, abolitionist)

"Success, a sort of suicide, is ruined by success." Young (Unknown)

"The graveyards are full of people the world could not do without." Elbert Hubbard (American author, editor, and printer)

"If a free society cannot help the many who are poor, it cannot save the few who are rich." John F. Kennedy. (American President)

"Enough's as good as a feast." Scottish Proverb

"In the history of mankind many republics have risen, have flourished for a less or greater time, and then have fallen because their citizens lost the power of governing themselves and thereby of governing their state; and in no way has this loss of power been so often and so clearly shown as in the tendency to turn the government into a government primarily for the benefit of one class instead of a government for the benefit of the people as a whole." Teddy Roosevelt (American President)

Chapter 10

Kant has approached this meaning of life search by asking three questions for us to answer. "What can we know?", "Given the limits of our reason, what ought we to do?", and "For what can we hope?" I am basically trying to answer all three of these questions. The individual points being made throughout this discourse are not complicated points—in part because I would be in over my own head with such an attempt, and in part because finding meaning in life would have to be straightforward enough so most humans could understand the path needed to follow. Whatever the meaning of life is, for any species, it cannot be something which is beyond the innate capability of the species except perhaps for a defective small few. If only Einsteins are capable of finding the meaning of life, then this whole discourse is irrelevant to most of us. **THERE IS CERTAINLY NO EVIDENCE THAT THE SMARTEST AMONGST US ARE THE MOST CONTENTED.**

For those people whose faith is based on inherited packaged dogmas, there is always pictured a God—after all the vindictiveness, punishments, and favoritism are ignored— who is a God of compassion, power, mercy, and brilliance. Most of the followers of packaged religion fear death immensely, prolong their lives as long as possible, and don't understand why God allows them to age and then die. This is, naturally, quite puzzling if we as individuals are important to God. But suppose God did create a system of life in which we did not age or die? What would be the purpose of living forever? It certainly wouldn't advance the evolutionary process, and where would the planet put all the people? And as for Heaven, are all species eligible for Heaven? Most probably believe only humans are, or at most, humans and their pets. But then, if humans in the future end up no longer the most advanced species, do humans lose Heaven and get replaced there by the newer more advanced species? Look, if humans didn't die, none of us would have been given the chance to be born—the earth would be too full. We pass through stages in our lives from formative, to productive, to terminational because this allows us different types of experiences at different ages. There is nothing cruel about death, death allows room for others to then exist. As was pointed out before, I didn't exist for millions of years. How do I feel about having been non existent for so long? I don't feel anything. It is hard to miss nothing. And it will be no harder to miss nothing again IF there is no Heaven.

If God's goal is to enable individual members of the human species to earn their way to a 'Heaven' after death, why would he allow anyone to die by accident, disease, or murder before having a decent chance to earn their way to Heaven? Or do those who die young go to Heaven by 'default'? If so, the fortunate die young, the smart kill themselves early on, and those who think they have earned their way to Heaven would be really eager in old age to die, would refuse medical measures to prolong their lives, and be like a kid on Christmas eve—just can't wait to receive, in this case, the gift of death. We don't really see much of that do we? Again, this doesn't mean there might not be some sort of

Heaven, but if there is one, it is beyond human comprehension. **FAITH, WE NEED REMEMBER—BY DEFINITION—DOES NOT MAKE ANYTHING A FACT**.

At the risk of being too repetitive, it seems obligatory to repeat, in a new-wrinkled way, that once we attempt to place ourselves at front and center of the evolutionary process we distort reality. By what line of reasoning can we declare God has given us dominion over any aspect of the evolutionary process, or that we are made in the image of God, or that God awaits our prayers to interfere with His own laws of the evolutionary process, or that our particular species has a Heaven after death awaiting us? If any of this is true it is certainly beyond the level of human reason to decipher it as true. That leaves inherited religious dogma as the only basis for it. It becomes a pure act of faith. Faith is a valued human trait. Nevertheless, this trait abused, can be used to bolster behaviors contrary to reality and contrary to the Golden Rule. The contention here is that no one can reach a high level of personal contentment if they deny reality or fail to reach their own potential ethical state (by following the Golden Rule). **REACHING A STATE OF CONTENTMENT IS NOT A CONSEQUENCE OF HAVING CHANGED THE WORLD AROUND US, BUT A CONSEQUENCE OF HAVING TRANSFORMED OUR OWN MINDS**.

Self-transformation is an arduous task. It requires dedicated adherence to reason, it requires patience, it requires controlling emotions—especially anger. When one is emotional, sound reasoning can be lost. There is a certain **EMOTIONAL DETACHMENT** required to fairly weigh matters before us. We all know how overindulgence in religious faith, patriotism, family loyalty, cultural bias, etc. can lead to unfairness, distrust, and intolerance. It is human to be prejudiced in these matters but it is working through our prejudices which helps put us on the long and hard road to contentment in our lives. The emotions most likely to interfere with rational thought appear to be anger, fear, and hope. All three of these emotions are necessary to our lives, but they have to be mastered. No-one whose life is dominated by any of these emotions can be contented. Of course there are times to be angry, times to be fearful and times to be hopeful. In terms of reaching a contented life all three can be hurdles necessary to overcome in order to achieve substantial contentment. One cannot become angry at diversity or you end up attempting to swim upstream against the whole evolutionary process. What is the point of flailing away against the very engine which drives God's evolutionary process? Hope is needed to keep us motivated but hope is not, by itself, any road to contentment. I can hope ever so hard that my favorite team wins the playoffs, but no one would mistake my hope as a state of contentment. I can hope very hard to become wealthy but no one is going to mistake this hope with a state of contentment. Hope is tied in with want. In fact, **THOSE WHO ARE HAPPY WITH LESS ARE MORE CONTENTED THAN THOSE WHO HAVE MUCH AND WANT MORE**. A lot of earned wealth is inter-digitally dovetailed with obsessive behavior. **OBSESSIVE BEHAVIOR IS NOT CONTENTMENT**. Fear may well have the worst impact on personal contentment.

A lot of religious fervor is tied to fear of death. It is far easier to accept that nothing in life seems to have any real permanence **EXCEPT** our own lives. **HOWEVER,** what kind of rational reason can there be to make ourselves the sole exception? I suppose, if we wish to insist we are the endpoint of the evolutionary process we can believe that, as the end point, our species has a special reward—everlasting life. The trouble with adopting this belief is that we end up with this intense fear of death. We say, or think often enough, that we are saved, but we also know this is a pure act of faith. As death approaches, the fear associated with a faith- based belief in Heaven creates considerable anxiety. Suppose it is not true? Most of us are aware our lives were not exactly lived according to the dictates of Christ, Buddha, Gandhi, Mohammed, etc. We have tried to serve two masters: the ethical principle of the Golden Rule and the mindset of modernism. This may well be why the intensely religious seem to have the greatest fear of death. They have staked everything on their personal salvation, but of course, having staked so much on this, as aging proceeds they realize soon the shit will hit the fan. Which of us, upon finding out we have terminal cancer, rushes home all excited about finally going to heaven? I haven't seen that yet. Many things we believe turn out to be incorrect; we learn to have hope about our beliefs but suspicion will always be there. People get married because they believe they truly love each other and they believe clergy when told 'what God has put together let no man put asunder'. Well, in this country, the divorce rate is about 50%. If their belief about a marriage ends up unfounded, then what about life after death? People who **HAVE ACCEPTED** the impermanence of their lives have no fear of death. They enjoy life while they can, and are ever so grateful for whatever luck comes their way, and any assistance received from others. It is a very fair system in this respect. **PEOPLE BUILD PEOPLE. SO, FOR US TO HAVE CONTENTED LIVES, HELP FROM OTHERS IS NEEDED,** and for us to be contented with our own life the inherent ethical nature of humans—the Golden Rule—must be a significant driving force in our lives. Thus, contentment can be considered a balanced equation between helping others and being helped. Contentment cannot be achieved by only one side of the equation. Helping others, in the context being used here, means others outside our own family or circle of friends. This is not to say one should not help family and friends, BUT to throw money at family members and friends, while others with far greater needs are mostly ignored, is an ethical failure. It is simply not rational, and most certainly self serving, to believe God favors us or our families, or our friends, or our nation etc. over others. It is hard to envision why so many people view God to be that way. If God is on anyone's side—which probably He is not—HE certainly would be on the side of those who make the greatest effort to help those most in need of help.

Would God really be impressed to find out we made a million dollars of excessive wealth and then gave most of it to our children instead of the least fortunate in life? **AREN'T ALL CHILDREN GOD'S CHILDREN?** On what logical basis are we to remotely conclude that our own children are more important to God than other children or, for that matter, any other humans?

This notion that it is ok to extract a lot of wealth from society and yet never return the excess back into society—specifically to help those with the greatest need—but instead try to give unearned wealth to adult offspring is simply self centered and unethical. It is also the direct opposite of the Golden Rule and the teachings of every major prophet in most religions. Can anyone logically imagine Jesus, for example, advising someone to give their excess wealth, upon death, to their own kids and not to those most in need of assistance? If everyone gave their excess wealth at some point in their lives to those most in need, there would be no people starving, no people homeless, no people dying from curable diseases, etc. Of course, it is far easier to pray to God to help these poor unfortunate souls. God does help—he gave the human species, through His evolutionary process, the ethical basis to help the less fortunate. If we, collectively, refuse to do this, it is not God's fault. In essence, a lot of people suffer from the 'family values' of others.

Achieving a meaningful life has been defined here as achieving a contented life. Whatever contentment is, it is not something we are born with as an innate condition. People do end up being contented in life without going through this elaborate musing as I am doing here. Most people learn and conclude things without writing everything out. That is just an oddity of my own nature. One would not likely find an abundance of contentment in one's formative years. I mean really, this is the period of time in which there are so many things to figure out. The formative years can be many things including exciting, fun, and meaningful. The productive years can be challenging, exciting, and economically rewarding. The first two stages of life kind of set the stage, or fail to set the stage, to achieving substantial contentment. **CONTENTMENT IS NOT ACHIEVED OVERNIGHT, THERE IS NO TIMETABLE FOR ACHIEVING IT, IT MAY NEVER BE ACHIEVED, AND, IF ACHIEVED, IT WILL BE A MATTER OF TO WHAT DEGREE.**

If reason and our innate understanding of ethics are the path to reaching contentment, this pathway is **TIME DEPENDENT**. That is, the improved scientific understanding of matters has grown dramatically over human history. Religion was really invented as a means to assuage our discomfort over understanding so little of the world. If we cannot actually know something, then we can at least believe in something. Many religious dogmas were developed out of scientific ignorance. As science developed more answers to more facets of life, religion, and science began to clash over time, at first violently, and now a lot more subtly. Major religions still retain some unbelievable dogmas, but most followers sort of pick and choose those which they choose to believe. For me, if any of the religious scriptures were indeed the word of God, there would certainly never be a need to revise them. The earth would still be flat, slavery okay, women subservient to men, sex only existent as a means of reproduction, stoning a good means of punishment, etc. Most religious scripture is an exercise in reasoned out ethics at a certain period of time. As time changes, human understanding of ethics changes with it. I mean, what else is new here? Everything changes with time. What has not changed with time is the Golden Rule. What varies is only the degree to which a person or nation or culture follows the Golden Rule. I don't know of any culture or time in human history which flat out denies that others count. The problem has always been that some count more than others for varied reasons and with varied consequences. The founders of our democracy declared all men were created equal, not in abilities, but in rights and justice owed them. Back then that was pretty much limited to land owning white men, providing in some cases they were not Catholic or Jewish. A couple of hundred years have passed and we still are adjusting our laws to implement a society in which all basic human rights are given to all people..

Some argue that if we cannot prove some religious beliefs then we should discard all of them. I don't personally buy that. Instead, I view this problem as using our best and most detached reasoning to formulate beliefs which are not absurd or illogical. When someone says, for example, that birth control is a sin, I wonder just what kind of logical reasoning produces such a belief? If reasonableness is not a prerequisite for our beliefs, then the door is open to believe just about anything. And some people do. The only thing they have is a hand on some sort of bible from which they believe certain passages on faith and then ignore other passages. When this scenario occurs, the most devout religious sect will find any kind of change in ethical behavior, like giving women the right to vote, an abomination. They will fight and fight—but because of the nature of evolution—they will lose; often not until the next generation will the change be accepted. Frankly, they are almost trapped into feeling this way. After all, if some portion of some bible is proven to be erroneous, then how much of the rest might not be true either? It is hard to say, "This is a sacred text, but only for today—tomorrow it may change." It just seems something that is indeed the 'Word" of God would never have a need to change. The fatal flaw in their beliefs is that hardly anyone seriously believes and follows every commandment in any religious text written thousands of years ago—written not by the prophet behind the commandments, but by certain followers decades later. This would be considered an absurd defense in any modern court room. Why would any reasonable person even think that God would attempt to communicate His laws in such a way—and a way in which the laws would only reach certain people via inheritance?

(12) Relevant Attestations:

"Only reason can convince us of those three fundamental truths without a recognition of which there can be no effective liberty; that what we believe is not necessarily true; that what we like is not necessarily good, and that all questions are open." Clive Bell (British art critic).

"But touch a solemn truth in collision with a dogma of a sect, though capable of the clearest proof, and you will soon find you have disturbed a nest, and the hornets will swarm about your eyes and hand, and fly into your face and eyes." John Adams (U.S. President)

"Every new truth which has been propounded has, for a time caused mischief; it has produced discomfort, and often unhappiness; sometimes disturbing social and religious arrangements.... And if the truth is very great as well as very uneasy; they flinch;

they cannot bear the sudden light; a general restlessness supervenes; the face of society is disturbed, or perhaps convulsed; old interests and old beliefs have been destroyed before new ones have been created. These symptoms are the precursors of revolution; they have preceded all the great changes through which the world has passed." Robert Browning (English poet)

"Man is a religious animal. He is the only religious animal. He is the only animal that has the True Religion—several of them. He is the only animal that loves his neighbors as himself and cuts his neighbor's throat if his theology isn't straight." Mark Twain (American writer)

"Religion has treated knowledge sometimes as an enemy, sometimes as a hostage; often as a captive and more often as a child; but knowledge has become of age and religion must either renounce her acquaintance, or introduce her as a companion and respect her as a friend." Charles Caleb Colton (English poet, essayist)

"Many people have looked upon Jesus as a true theist, whose religion has been by degrees corrupted. Indeed, in the books which contain the law which is attributed to him, there is no mention either of worship, or of priests, or of sacrifices, or of sufferings, or of the greater part of the doctrines of actual Christianity, which has become the most prejudicial of the superstitions of the earth." Denis Diderot (French philosopher, atheist)

"Think of the dull functioning of dogma, age after age. How many millions have been led shunted along dogmatic runways from the dark into the dark again....endless billions, and the gates, dogma, ignorance, vice, cruelty, seize them and clamp this or that band upon their brains." Theodore Dreiser (American writer).

"Science without religion is lame, religion without science is blind." Albert Einstein (German born, Swiss-American scientist)

"Agnosticism, in fact, is not a creed, but a method, the essence of which lies in the rigorous application of a single principle. That principle is of great antiquity; it is as old as Socrates, as old as the writer who said, 'Try all things, hold fast by that which is good'; it is the foundation of the Reformation, which simply illustrated the axiom that every man should be able to give a reason for the faith that is in him; it is the great principle of Descartes; it is the fundamental axiom of modern science. Positively the principle may be expressed: In matters of the intellect, follow your reason as far as it will take you, without regard to any other consideration. And negatively, in matters of the intellect, do not pretend that conclusions are certain which are demonstrated or demonstrable. That I take to be the agnostic faith, which if a man keep whole and undefiled, he shall not be ashamed to look the universe in the face, whatever the future may have in store for him." Thomas Henry Huxley (British biologist)

"They (the clergy) believe that any portion of power confided to me, will be exerted in opposition to their schemes. And they believe rightly; for I have sworn upon the alter of God eternal hostility against every form of tyranny over the mind of man." Thomas Jefferson (United States President)

"In every country and in every age, the priest has been hostile to liberty. He is always in alliance with the despot...they have perverted the purest religion ever preached to man into mystery and jargon, unintelligible to all mankind, and therefore the safer engine for their purpose." Thomas Jefferson (U.S. President)

"That they (the dogmas of religion) do little harm is not true. Opposition to birth control makes it impossible to solve the population problem and therefore postpones indefinitely all chance of world peace." Bertrand Russell (British mathematician, philosopher)

"The bad thing about all religions is that, instead of being able to confess their allegorical nature, they have to conceal it; accordingly, they parade their doctrine in all seriousness as true sensu proprio, and as absurdities form an essential part of these doctrines, you have the great mischief of a continual fraud." Arthur Schopenhauer (German philosopher)

"The church has stood, a rock colossus of bigotry, in the path of ten thousand reforms. Sane efforts to legalize birth control, the dissemination of birth control information—the publication of psychological and physical sex information....myriad attempts by sane men acting sanely on real problems—have been fought down by church-frightened legislatures and church dominated courts." Philip Wylie (American writer)

"Every day people are straying away from the church and going back to God." Lenny Bruce (Jewish American comedian and social critic)

"I think religion is often very different from spirituality. Religion is often about rules and people trying to control our lives who are actually very unspiritual.....God can be found anywhere, and in fact, everywhere. And you don't necessarily need a religious dogma to get you to spirituality." Darren Aronosfsky (American film director)

Chapter 11

CONTENTMENT IS NOT SOMETHING THAT CAN BE CREATED IN A SOCIAL VACUUM. There has to be some sort of supporting social relationship which fits the personality of the person in question. No man is an island unto himself. **IN A VERY PERSONAL WAY WE NEED OTHERS FOR US TO BECOME WHAT WE ARE CAPABLE OF BECOMING.** It may take a village, as Hilliary Clinton suggests, or it may take a grandmother, as Terrell Owens credits. The Golden Rule reflects that necessity. These relationships cannot be governed solely by natural attraction, however. When this happens you get tightly knit units of people devoted to each other, but hostile or indifferent to everyone else—varied versions of the 'family values' mentality. A hostile social environment does not create a flourishing society. The ability for complex reasoning is both an advantage and a disadvantage. This complex reasoning can be used for good or bad, to bring people together or to divide people into groups. Clearly, if it is diversity which drives the evolutionary process, then any inability of a species like humans to appreciate, and feel comfortable with, diversity spells trouble—for everyone involved. **IT IS IN EVERYONE'S BEST INTEREST TO EXTEND NATURAL SYMPATHIES TO DIVERSE GROUPS OF PEOPLE**

IN ORDER TO CONSTRUCT STABLE, JUST, SOCIETIES. Organized religion, in more cases than not, has failed to accept diversity of beliefs. The reality is that when we are kind to those quite diverse in some way compared to ourselves, the object of our kindness realizes the extent of our effort, and invariably he/she responds with an extra effort of friendliness in return. One can be Hitlertarian in approach to others or Obamaterian. Most everyone is somewhere in between.

Immanuel Kant made an interesting challenge about the meaning of life: "Dare to Know." In Kant's view we are born immature, and, to achieve what I call contentment in life, one must pass from this personal immaturity to maturity. During the formative years we have books which tell us what we should know, spiritual advisors who control our conscience, doctors to decide our health, political leaders to decide our politics, etc. **THIS IS A STAGE OF LIFE IN WHICH WE ARE COMPLICIT IN OUR OWN JUVENILIZATION.** At this stage, a lot of our thinking is done by others for us. And thus, to mature, we need "dare to know". Gandhi and Buddha were of the same notion. When we become adults, however, we should question everything we have ever been taught, and let our minds test all of it through our own rational reasoning. To be immature and mindlessly obedient to others is to stifle our own intellectual potential for reaching our own conclusions about the experience called life. Just as people who live off inherited money often feel inadequate without a lot of personal achievement in their lives, so do those whose conclusions on matters of understanding life are handed to them by others. It is hard to end up contented if our achievements in life and our interpretations of life are not a product of our own efforts and intellectual reasoning. To answer the question "Why?" by saying "because "X" says so", is about the fastest way to a bored, discontented life. **HUMANS**

NEED FREEDOM, JUSTICE, ASSISTANCE, AND COURAGE TO DEVELOP THEIR OWN POTENTIAL IN LIFE. People admire the words of the song "I Did it My Way" because they kind of do know that is the charge given to all of us in life. All we have ever been given is a chance—a chance to achieve something, and to achieve it in a way which will bring contentment, which means we have to, in the end, do it our way—constrained only by the Golden Rule. To never live our own lives, to robotize our existence via blind obedience to culture, to inherited religion, to tradition, to race, to majority rule, to our emotions, to our wants, etc. is to render achieving a contented life moot. It simply cannot be done.

Relevant Attestations (13):

"To be yourself in a world that is constantly trying to make you something else is the greatest accomplishment." Ralph Waldo Emerson (American essayist and poet)

"I think the reward for conformity is that everyone likes you except yourself." Rita Mae Brown (American writer)

"The individual has always had to struggle to keep from being overwhelmed by the tribe. If you try it, you will be lonely often, and sometimes frightened. But no price is too high to pay for the privilege of owning yourself." Friedrich Nietzsche (German philosopher)

"Why are you trying so hard to fit in, when you're born to stand out" Oliver James (Clinical psychologist)

"About all you can do in life is be who you are. Some people will love your you. Most will love you for what you can do for them, and some won't like you at all." Rita Mae Brown (American writer)

"In order to be irreplaceable, one must always be different." Coco Chanel (French fashion designer)

"The things that make me different are the things that make me." A.A. Milne (British author)

"I am not in this world to live up to your expectations and you're not in this world to live up to mine." Bruce Lee (Martial artist)

"I often warn people: 'Somewhere along the way someone is going to tell you, 'There is no "I" in team.' What you should tell them is, 'Maybe not. But there is an "I" in independence, individuality and integrity.' George Carlin (American humorist)

"Never be bullied into silence. Never allow yourself to be made a victim. Accept no one's definition of your life; define yourself." Harvey Fierstein (American actor and playwright)

"I've come to believe that each of us has a personal calling that's as unique as a fingerprint—and that the best way to succeed is to discover what you love and then find a way to offer it to others in the form of service, working hard, and also allowing the energy of the universe to lead you." Oprah Winfrey (American TV talk show host)

"I wore black because I liked it. I still do, and wearing it still means something to me. It's still my symbol of rebellion—against a stagnant status quo, against our hypocritical houses of God, against people whose minds are closed to others' ideas." Johnny Cash (American singer)

"I won't tell you that the world matters nothing, or the world's voice, or the voice of society. They matter a good deal. They matter far too much. But there are moments when one has to choose between living one's own life, full, entirely, completely—or dragging out some false, shallow, degrading existence that the world in its hypocrisy demands. You have that moment now. Choose!" Oscar Wilde (Irish writer and poet).

"Humanity's most valuable assets have been the non-conformists. Were it not for the non-conformists, he who refuses to be satisfied to go along with the continuance of things as they are, and insists upon attempting to find new ways of bettering things, the world would have known little progress indeed." Josiah William Gitt (American writer)

"The great law of culture is: Let each become all that he was created capable of being: expand, if possible to his full growth; and show himself at length in his own shape and stature be these what they may." Thomas Carlyle (Scottish writer and historian)

"Where all think alike, no one thinks very much." Walter Lippman (American writer and political commentator)

"Differences of opinion are opportunities for learning, new footholds for change and growth, valuable exercises for minds grown sluggish and characters grown smug." Sydney Harris (American essayist and drama critic)

"Consistency requires you to be as ignorant today as you were a year ago." Bernard Berenson (American art historian)

"A foolish consistency is the hobgoblin of little minds, adored by little statesmen and philosophers and divines." Ralph Waldo Emerson (American essayist and poet)

Chapter 12

A certain lyric in a popular song has always intrigued me over the years: **"HOW MANY TIMES CAN A MAN TURN HIS HEAD, AND PRETEND THAT HE JUST DOESN'T SEE?"** I sense this has a lot to do with achieving contentment in our lives. We all have done this pretension, and some times en masse—with respect to slavery, women's right to vote, the Vietnam War, refusal to grant civil rights to those deprived of them, etc. When we turn our heads away from matters which we have the ability to reason against, we bury this pretension in our psyche. It then remains as some sort of baggage which we carry around inside our very inner self, baggage which makes it difficult to achieve any full contented state. **IT ALWAYS COMES BACK TO THE FACT THAT IN MANY CASES WE REALLY DO KNOW BETTER, BUT PREFER TO REMAIN OBEDIENT TO TRADITION, TO CULTURE, TO POLITICAL LABELS, TO INHERITED RELIGIOUS PRINCIPLES, TO JUVENILE PREJUDICES, ETC.** In other cases we rationalize away doing wrong instead of right because doing wrong gains us immediate material gain, power gain, or popularity gain. **NEITHER MATERIAL, POWER, OR POPULARITY GAIN CAN BRING CONTENTMENT.** Of course, this is true only past a certain level of material gain, power gain, or popularity gain. A child who steals a cupcake because he/she is impoverished and hungry is not really a criminal. It is instead the society and all those who support such a society who are the guilty ones—because we all know that NO CHILD should be left hungry while 30% of others are overweight—and even if no one else is overweight.

All of us who supported the War in Vietnam are guilty of complicity in the deaths of 35,000 American young men and 2 million Vietnamese. And of course all those who supported Al Qaeda are guilty of killing 2500 Americans in the Trade Tower bombings. And this goes on and on. All those who support their own right to drink alcohol and smoke cigarettes, and fail to support the right of others to smoke marijuana, are guilty by complicity of putting tens of thousands of young people in jail for smoking pot or selling it, at a cost of $30,000 a year to keep them in jail, not to mention making it almost a certainty that the chances of these young people becoming productive citizens goes down the drain in the process. Our political War on Drugs, instead of a program for medical help to drug addiction or addiction of any sort, has helped destroy our inner cities, and created an environment for the hapless young people left in the ruins to make some money selling pot, the main engine for the drug trade. The tyranny of the majority has never been so evident in American politics as in recreational drug abuse. The two most popular recreational drugs are nicotine and alcohol, so they are legal even though their physiological toxicity to the body far exceeds the toxicity of marijuana, a drug used early on mostly by hispanics.

This exercise of turning our heads and pretending we just don't see is not just an impediment to our own level of personal contentment, but suicidal to the welfare of some others. It is not like our personal actions or inactions by themselves can reverse the evolutionary process. Our individual actions cannot. **BUT**, our personal actions or inactions can determine the level of personal contentment we achieve and others might be able to achieve. This evolutionary process, governed by God's laws, ensures that in the long run progress continues, not in a straight line but forward eventually. So when people fail to adhere to the Golden Rule, individually or en masse, it is not a failure of the evolutionary process itself, but a failure for all those who have stifled their own ethical development by their actions. The only hope for them is some sort of irrational belief that despite avoiding the Golden Rule, some sort of contentment awaits them in Heaven. Only if we think the Golden Rule is not the ethical basis for human life, can we, by any logic, think a Heaven awaits us, in this life, or an afterlife, by ignoring the Golden Rule. We always need keep in mind that ethics involves right and wrong—and right and wrong involves punishment and reward. **WE DON'T BEHAVE ETHICALLY FOR THE HELL OF IT. WE EXPECT TO BE REWARDED FOR DOING RIGHT**. Personal contentment is the reward.

It was said before that no man is an island. All of us know the value of friendship in our lives, with the word 'friend' being used in the broadest sense. A parent can be our friend, a teacher, a spouse, a boss, a peer, a pet, and so it goes on and on. Friendships are not all of the same make-up. The best friendship is often described as one in which the two friends fit each other like a hand in a glove. This can be true of parent-child, pet and owner, married partners, social friends, etc. But **IN A WORLD OF CHANGE, WHAT ONCE WAS A CLOSE FIT MAY END UP NOT SO GOOD A FIT FOR ANY NUMBER OF REASONS**. It often doesn't mean anyone is to blame, nor does it mean the friendship failed. Friendships mold and change us, and few things in our lives prove to be more relevant to our future contentment than close friends, past and present. If a friendship fades, the benefits gained from the friendship remain. The good memories are still there. Nothing causes a friendship to fade more than distance. Close friendships tend to be between people who share a lot of relevancy in their lives at a particular point in time. **FOR US TO ACHIEVE CONTENTMENT, FRIENDS ARE NEEDED**. What can be overlooked, however, are the other kinds of friendships needed for personal contentment to settle in our psyche. The Golden Rule, by definition, **REQUIRES** that we befriend, in some form or fashion, the least fortunate in the world. This friendship can be direct, but most likely will not be direct. Sharing our wealth, past the basics we need to live, with the least fortunate, is a type of friendship. Supporting politics which are beneficial to the least fortunate is a type of friendship. Personally befriending those in our own lives who most need some friendship is a kind of friendship. Giving those with little confidence or skills the chance to get a useful job is a form of friendship. Befriending the ugly is a kind of friendship. Befriending those without charming personalities is a kind of friendship, and befriending those whose harmless peculiarities set them up to be targets of social derision is a kind of friendship. When we form those kind of friendships we are on the road to becoming a contented person. Remember, **ETHICS IS AN INBORN POTENTIAL—IN OTHER WORDS IT HAS A GENETIC BASIS—** a human characteristic, and failure to practice and develop this ethical potential, because of the neural network developmental process of man, means contentment cannot then be generated. In the terminational years what is left from the good friendships in earlier years are the uplifting memories and lessons learned. Those who failed, for whatever reasons, to establish a lot of good friendships in their formative and productive years, will find friendships established in the terminational years to be even more difficult.

If one ever takes the time to observe most elderly people chatting with each other, the apparent dullness of the conversation is enough to put one to sleep. I can remember sitting at a dining table in an assisted living complex with my mother and observing the loudness of the silence. If I asked a question of someone they would try, in a friendly way, to answer, but it was clear this effort I was demanding was not all that welcome. Even though these people saw each other every day they had little in common, and all of them were but a shadow of those who used to be far more vibrant and mentally sharp persons. My mother was a fairly contented person in her latter years, and when she got deaf enough for conversation to be difficult, I used to just mention a name from her past and let her talk about her memories from that past. It was those good memories from her past which enabled her to be more contented in her terminal years. What I am saying here is that **GOOD MEMORIES ARE MONEY IN THE BANK, TO BE DRAWN UPON LATER IN LIFE, WHEN THERE IS PRECIOUS LITTLE ELSE TO SUSTAIN A CONTENTED STATE.**

TOLERANCE FOR DIVERSITY IS EXPRESSED BY RESPECTING DIVERSITY. John Stuart Mill was the first to emphasize, in concise language, the need for individual liberty. I simply extend this to mean one cannot reach contentment (the individual goal to give life its meaning) without respecting diversity. According to Mill the only time society has a right to suppress individual freedom is for self-protection. As Mill said, **"OVER HIMSELF, OVER HIS OWN BODY AND MIND, THE INDIVIDUAL IS SOVEREIGN."** Mill's concern was with the tyranny of the majority: "Society....practices a social tyranny more formidable than many kinds of political oppression, since—it leaves fewer means of escape, penetrating more deeply into the details of life and enslaving the soul itself." We are exposed to social tyranny through politics, religious dogmas, advertising—all of which insist to us that we must believe, think, dress, or behave in certain ways if we are to be accepted members of the 'majority' mindset. Evolution depends on competition and change. **PLURALISM IN SOCIETY IS THE ENGINE WHICH GENERATES EVOLUTIONARY PROGRESS**. If we sometimes WON'T "dare to think", then those who do think force us to defend current practices and this process may give us a clearer picture of what we ourselves think and why. "My way or the highway" is an oxymoronic phrase. Different views or customs may be better for different people. Failure to understand this impacts heavily on our disposition. If one cannot accept diversity, change, and the real position of our own selves in the evolutionary process we simply cannot be contented. **MANY OF THE 'HOT BUTTON' ISSUES THAT POLITICIANS USE TO GET ELECTED PREY ON THOSE WHO CANNOT RESPECT DIVERSITY OF OPINIONS, CULTURE, RELIGION, ETHNICITY**, etc. Some people see diversity and individuality as factors which promote disunity and conflict. Mill insists that diversity promotes progress and originality, making evolutionary progress possible. Truth, in the evolutionary process, always wins out. When we walk around with braces on our brains, our minds buried in faith based beliefs of the past, every battle won to defend injustices to others is but temporary. To deny this is to be ignorant of history.

Relevant Attestations: (14)

"Civilizations should be measured by the degree of diversity attained and the degree of unity retained." W.H. Auden (English/American poet)

"Human diversity makes tolerance more than a virtue; it makes it a requirement for survival." Rene Dubos (American microbiologist)

"When you reduce life to black and white, you never see rainbows." Rachael Houston

"Diversity is not about how we differ. Diversity is about embracing one another's uniqueness." Ola Joseph (Nigerian author)

"If we cannot end now our differences, at least we can help make the world safe for diversity." John Kennedy (American President)

"If man is to survive, he will have learned to take a delight in the essential differences between men and between cultures. He will learn that differences in ideas and attitudes are a delight, part of life's exciting variety, not something to fear." Gene Roddenberry (American TV screen writer and producer)

"What we have to do….is to find a way to celebrate our diversity and debate our differences without fracturing our communities." Hillary Clinton (American Senator and Secretary of State)

"Diversity may be the hardest thing for a society to live with, and perhaps the most dangerous thing for a society to be without." William Sloane Coffin Jr. (American clergyman and Peace Activist)

"Difference is of the essence of humanity. Difference is an accident of birth and it should therefore never be the source of hatred or conflict. The answer to difference is to respect it. Therein lies a most fundamental principle of peace: respect for diversity. John Hume (Irish politician)

"At bottom every man knows well enough that he is a unique being, only once on this earth; and by no extraordinary chance will such a marvelously picturesque piece of diversity in unity as he is, ever be put together a second time." Friedrich Nietzche (German philosopher)

"The legitimate powers of government extend to such acts only as are injurious to others. But it does me no injury for my neighbor to say there are twenty Gods, or no God. It neither picks my pocket nor breaks my leg." Thomas Jefferson (U.S. President)

"Everybody's journey is individual. You don't know with whom you're going to fall in love.....if you fall in love with the wrong color, wrong religion, wrong sex—you fall in love." James Baldwin (American novelist, poet, social critic)

Chapter 13

Accepting the realities and significance of our own lives in God's created process of evolution has been emphasized as necessary to reach a contented state of mind in life. Fear of death is also an issue that can thwart contentment. If death is not a natural part of life what the hell is? We can try to isolate death as some sort of anomalous moment at which we cease to live, but this is patently ridiculous. In the broadest sense, life is a continuum. The DNA which was assembled to generate our own existence just keeps on reassembling, as it has for millions of years, with new patterns of assemblage and thus new unique forms of life. All of us came from pre-existing living cells (So much for this nonsense of when our lives began). There are some who spend an inordinate amount of time trying to define exactly at what moment, under prescribed physical conditions, death has occurred. Nothing could be more silly or inane or disingenuous than this kind of emphasis. From the moment we are born, change is the operative word throughout life. **THERE IS NO SINGULAR DEFINABLE 'I" AT ANY POINT IN OUR LIVES.** The 'I' of my youth has been nonexistent for a long, long time. The 'I' of me as an athlete has been gone for a long, long time. The 'I' of me as a sexual object has been gone for a long,

long time. The 'I' of a person as a parent dissipates with time. Every aspect of our being changes with time. We do, in reality, die a thousand deaths, of one ilk or another, over the years. Every friend or loved one who dies takes a part of us with them. **DEATH IS, FROM ANY PRACTICAL DEFINITION, A LONG DRAWN-OUT PROCESS THAT STARTS WITH BIRTH**. To fear death is to fear life itself, or more accurately, to not really understand the nature of life. When people believe for sure they will have a life in heaven, I always wonder which—of the many lives they lived over the years—will be resurrected in heaven?

But these thoughts are of no matter—about as helpful to anything as wondering what my life would have been like had I been the most handsome person in the world, or the smartest, or the most popular singer, etc. There is nothing wrong with day-dreaming unless the day dreams become some sort of false reality in our lives. **EVERYTHING WE EVER WERE, OR ARE, IS GOING TO DISAPPEAR**. In the river of life only fools spend a lot of time trying to swim upstream. Not only is this exhausting and fruitless, but you end up downstream anyway, just all upset you couldn't go back upstream. I love to write out my thoughts (a real understatement), neither a good nor a bad trait, just a personal trait. At my age I realize this ability to express myself in writing, or to think clearly enough to generate any thoughts worth writing about, will dissipate in the near future as I proceed through the dying process. **DEATH, FOR THE MOST PART, IS BY A THOUSAND CUTS**. If change is one of the operative laws of evolution how can death be by any other means? The neat thing about change is that we all get to experience and adjust to new realities all our lives. There is no same old, same old, same old. **"EVERY DAY IS THE TOMORROW WE WORRIED ABOUT YESTERDAY"** (Ann Brashares). Change is a blessing, it brings new challenges, new understandings, new circumstances, new people in our lives, new hurdles, new successes, new failures, just new, new, new.

The real question–for each of us to answer in his or her own way is this: what sort of activities in our lives will maximize contentment? One could be exceptionally silly here and wish to win the lottery, to become materially rich, or more powerful, etc. We have already established where all this leads and it never brings contentment. For me, a day is wasted if I have not learned something new about something of substance, or felt, through nature, a deeper connection to this whole process called life, or enjoyed a good meal, or read a good book, or listened to my favorite music, or had friendly banter or discussions with interesting people. Every time I feel I understand something better about the world in which I live, or those around me live in this world, I feel more contented. **A WASTED DAY IS ONE IN WHICH EVERYTHING IS ABOUT MUNDANE MATTERS**, trivial conversations, and, worst of all, **BEING TRAPPED INTO TIME- CONSUMING BATTLES OVER TRIVIAL MATTERS**. That is the kind of thing we do when we are young—as half-assed, short-sighted, insecure trolls.

Contentment, to some debatable degree, depends on being attuned to our own individuality, **WITHIN THE LIMITS OF THE GOLDEN RULE**. The Golden Rule is not some arbitrary concept created by reason alone. Like other human characteristics such as the ability to laugh, to speak, and to walk upright **OUR ETHICAL NATURE IS A GENETICALLY IMPRINTED HUMAN TRAIT**. The Golden Rule simply condenses the nature of human ethics into a verbal description. We can live our own lives based on our own peculiar personalities, or we can live our lives as puppets, our thoughts and actions dictated by others. These others can be parents, bosses, spouses, friends, inherited religious dogmas, political dogmas, etc. The nature of diversity, one of the key factors in the evolutionary process, is such that individuality must be respected and protected. If one's goal is a contented life then we need be controlled by creativity, responsibility, authenticity, spontaneity, fairness, and honesty—not be puppets of some inherited dogmas, customs, prejudices, and systems of the past. This is not to suggest a life of trashing the past, **BUT A LIFE OF OUR OWN WHICH WILL CONTRIBUTE TO UPGRADING THE PAST. We all, TO REACH CONTENTMENT**, must represent something besides the demands of others. To develop our own potentials in various areas of life we need guard against too much daily clutter with meaningless banter, minor details, and inane amusements via varied gadgets. When we start to **CONFUSE AMUSEMENT WITH CONTENTMENT**, the latter may never be reached. Inheriting money, titles, social position, etc. will never bring real contentment. **NO ONE CAN GIVE YOU CONTENTMENT**—just ask the kids of the wealthy. Contentment is a product of personal development, and only that achieved with our own effort, sometimes with the assistance from others, can give any meaning to our lives. Again,"**DARE TO THINK**". Anyone can believe most anything and some do, but only those whose beliefs, which are based on rational reasoning, can achieve satisfaction. The example I like to use most is the Vietnam War. So many of us back then, including Barry Goldwater and myself, simply accepted the need to attack Vietnam because authority figures, political and religious, said we needed to. Here was a country which had never attacked anyone, had been controlled by other countries for endless decades, had never committed acts of terrorism against anyone anywhere; and yet we attacked and killed 2 million Vietnamese. With all our military might we lost that war, and we well deserved to lose it, if any form of justice were to prevail. It was a lesson I never forgot. I had the innate reasoning power at the time to know this venture was wrong WRIT large, but I instead let a 'system' (blind patriotism) and others dictate my feelings. Every time our thoughts and actions are dictated by outsiders and blind dogmas, we fail to progress towards a life of contentment. If you don't live your 'own' life, what personal meaning can life possibly have? **CONTENTMENT IS SOMETHING THAT COMES FROM WITHIN, NOT SOMETHING WHICH OTHERS CAN BESTOW UPON US.** Those who depend too much on others to amuse and support them, will have a really rough time when all these amusements and 'others' fall by the wayside due to distance, death, changing personalities, changing situations, etc. The terminational years, for this crowd, is brutal. Living is personal, very personal, and so is dying. **EVERYONE DIES 'ALONE'.** Even a huge adoring mob cannot reverse this, do the dying for you, make dying a new beginning of anything. Just as there is a time for flowers to wither and die, we too are destined to wither and die. Of course we wish otherwise, but there is no logical or reasonable basis to think that we, out of all the evolved individuals of any species in God's created evolutionary process, will live for eternity. That is a stretch and I think most people, in moments of reality, understand that.

Thus far I have postulated that the meaning of life is found in contentment, that contentment comes from within, that no man is an island, that our innate understanding of the Golden Rule is involved, and that this Golden Rule is a two way street. In the first two phases of life, the formative and productive stages, we tend to control our friendships as much as we can. We are more selective about whom we befriend and more demanding on what is required of someone else to merit our friendship. As observed, friendships often don't last forever for any number of reasons, not the least of these is the death of those once close to us. To a non-measurable degree, the level of contentedness arrived at by our terminational years determines the depth of our loss of so many who once were our 'friends'. This includes parents, spouses, social friends—the whole bag here. In the absence of contentment these losses are a source of persistent regret and anguish. If we never have come to accept death, change, and diversity, the loss of friends is inconsolable. We have been left 'on our own' and unprepared to handle this more solitary existence. As I have aged I am less selective about who can be my friend, demand less of a friend, focus more on those who need a friend, and follow my own interests as independently as possible. For example, you learn you can go to a museum without needing someone to go with you, that you can concentrate on your own interests in a museum better in the absence of others, that you can go to a restaurant because you just feel like having a particular kind of food without feeling you have to convince others they also feel a need to want that kind of food, etc. I also feel less compelled to demand much from others—to subject them to the 'or else' game.

IF SOMEONE FEELS A NEED TO DISTANCE THEMSELVES FROM US, WE SHOULD BE INCLINED TO LET THEM GO, WITHOUT WORRYING ABOUT THE NUANCES OF THEIR INCLINATION. Most of these frictional interactions are over personality, not blatant mistreatment. Diversity, by its very nature, comes with discordant personalities. If the Golden Rule is not being violated, then we all have the right to engage or not engage with someone as the moment dictates. Life is never a circumstance with everyone on the same wave length. The terminational years, if contented, are more selfish than the earlier two phases of life. Without a state of contentment in our terminational years we become a pest, spending an inordinate amount of time bothering others for them to cater to our needs. We might succeed to a certain degree in that others often feel an obligation to be 'respectful to' the elderly, and with enough nudging or begging they may oblige us a certain percentage of the time. This kind of tug of war doesn't bring contentment at all; it brings frustration and anger—feelings that we are alone and deserted by those who should care more about us, resentful that their attentions are elsewhere.

If the operative word in God's evolutionary process is change, then we need to adapt our own lives accordingly. Change is not just something that happens from generation to generation but something that happens in all of us as we experience life. We are never the same person in our terminational years as we were in our productive years or formative years. **IF WE CANNOT ACCEPT CHANGE IN OURSELVES AS WE EXPERIENCE LIFE AND GAIN A LARGER KNOWLEDGE BASE, THEN CONTENTMENT WILL BE ELUSIVE.** Not everything dumped in our laps in our formative years by others–by parents, by religious dogma, by culture, by environment. etc. is necessarily true. Some people spend a great deal of energy insisting whatever was inculcated in their minds by others in their formative years must be true forever more. In general I guess these people are bedrock conservatives. Any change for them is painful, if not impossible. **THESE ARE THE FAITH-BASED CABALS**.

To use reason as the basis for changes in ourselves is a sign of healthy maturation. This means we have to let go of a lot of our past. Most of us owe a lot to our parents and yet they usually die before we do and the loss is real. Of course as soon as we leave our formative years and embark on our productive years our parents are replaced, in varying degrees, by other influences. If not, contentment will be more difficult, as it always will be when we are tied to our past too strongly. Parents also have the need to let go of children after their formative years. Some parents just can't let go and this makes contentment for them in their terminational years more difficult. Again, whenever any of us depends too much on others to give us contentment, it is going to be a bumpy and unfulfilling ride. Contentment comes from within, not from without. The contented parent does the best he/she can and lets go. To tie our contentment to the fate of others is a risky and often unrewarding exercise.

Pets provide contentment and they will die. They better not be our only source of contentment. Friendships change because people change, distances change, current involvements change, and situations change. There is an old saying, **"GOD GIVES US OUR RELATIVES. THANK GOD WE CAN CHOOSE OUR FRIENDS."** (Ethal Watts Mumford) But we have to be careful with the word choose. Of course it is ethically true that we have a right to choose whom we marry. Even so, **MOST PEOPLE, IF THEY COULD REALLY CHOOSE WHOM THEY MARRY, WOULD BE MARRIED TO SOMEONE ELSE**. The choice has to be mutual. If we are shown a pile of shoes, all different styles and sizes, and told we can choose any pair of shoes for ourselves, in the end we have to settle for a pair of shoes that fit. Same with friendships. We might want to take the prettiest girl to the prom but the reality of our own looks precludes that. We may choose the most personable person to be our friend but our own personality may preclude that. Feelings prevail in choosing friends. Over time feelings can change. That is just the way it is, there do not have to be evil forces at work. We have to let go sometimes with friendships. **PERFORMING ENDLESS TAP DANCES TO PRESERVE A FRIENDSHIP WILL NOT LIKELY SAVE REAL FRIENDSHIPS AND WILL MOST LIKELY GENERATE CONSIDERABLE DISCONTENTMENT**. We all better have other ways to achieve contentment than to depend on others, even friends, to be the source of our contentment. All these factors mentioned here are important parts of our lives and contribute to contentment because they enable us to change as a consequence of our involvement with them. Prejudices are not people, but they are stumbling blocks to contentment also. To the extent diversity is annoying, contentment is limited. It will be hard to be contented when we feel we there are so many annoying diverse people in existence.

In the terminational years we are in the grandstand, no longer on the playing field; we need to accept that, to enjoy that, to feel the freedom that comes with having graduated from the 'rat race', to have the time—finally, to put all the pieces of life's puzzle together. We all learn a lot from the first two phases of life and yet, if health permits, our terminational years enable us to finally see the forest for the sake of the trees. This cannot be done in a non-contented state of mind. If we have been lucky enough in life to have achieved reasonable goals, to have been helped by others, and to have been helpful to others less fortunate, then there is no rational basis to be discontented in our terminational years. I mean, what the hell more could we have asked for in God's evolutionary process driven by chance, change, diversity, and environment? No one is forcing us to stay in the game. We can, if our cards are bad enough, fold at any time, not withstanding the notion of so many that God is toying with us personally, even to the extent of telling us exactly how and when we are to die. Clearly anyone can believe God is so involved with us individually, **BUT** this would then make God some sort of sadist–like the congregation members who told their their clergyman, lying in bed paralyzed from a stroke, "God is not through with you yet". I still wonder what kind of God they believe in Who would participate in such deliberate torture. In the past, people had their stroke or heart attack or cancer and just died rather quickly. Today you could be dragged through medical hell for months, even years, sometimes decades, before the torture ends- **–EVEN IF** you insist you have had enough, that you would like to be put to death peacefully, with a certain degree of dignity. Too often it matters little; **SOMEONE ELSE'S RELIGIOUS BELIEFS VIA GOVERNMENT LAW** will leave you in a tortured, unhappy state until 'God decides it is time for you to go'. These others have become virtual Gods of Death. This is nonsense elevated to insanity. If we think God decides when and how we go, then we need just stop interfering with man-made devices and medicines to keep our lives going. Who are we to be interfering with God's will? Religious canon can be seeped in a good amount of dooziness, but then we invariably see this most clearly in someone else's religious canon.

(15) Relevant attestations:

"It's not that I am afraid to die. I just don't want to be there when it happens." Woody Allen (U.S. film producer and actor)

"Old men are twice children." Aristophanes (Athenian poet, dramatist)

"When you are no longer what you were, there is no reason left for being alive." Marcus Tullius Cicero (Roman Orator, poet, statesman)

"Thus that which is the most awful of evils, death, is nothing to us, since when we exist there is no death, and when there is death we do not exist." Epictetus (Greek philosopher)

"The goal of all life is death." Sigmund Freud (Austrian psychologist)

"I am about to take my last voyage, a great leap in the dark." Thomas Hobbes (English philosopher)

"We are all under the sentence of death, but with a sort of indefinite reprieve." Victor Hugo (French poet, novelist, dramatist)

"Living is not the good, but living well. The wise man therefore lives as long as he should, not as long as he can. He will think of life in terms of quality, not quantity." Lucius Annaeus Seneca (Spanish born Roman statesman, philosopher)

"Age steals away all things, even the mind." Virgil (Roman poet)

"Time goes, you say? Ah no!!! Alas, time stays, we go." Dobson (American evangelist, psychologist)

"Whatever begins, also ends." Seneca (Roman philosopher and statesman)

"Some die too young and some die too old; the precept sounds strange, but die at the right time." Friedrich Nietzsche (German philosopher and writer)

"When I've learned enough to really live I'll be old enough to die." Ferlin Husky (American singer)

"Why live on and on anyway? If you live long enough everything in life you value becomes sullied." (Unknown)

"Medicine should be used not for the further extension of the life of the aged, but only for the full achievement of a natural and fitting life span and thereafter for the relief of suffering..... there will be better ways in the future to spend our money than on indefinitely extending the life of the elderly." Daniel Callahan (philosopher and co-founder of Hastings Center)

"It is gratifying to know that new medical procedures which permit prolongation of life are constantly being discovered, but frightening to realize the extent to which each achievement adds to the medical load. In the light of these facts, there is reason to fear that even the wealthiest economies may not be able to carry forever the enormous burden created by the scientific advances that permit 'medicated survival'." Rene Dubos (American microbiologist)

"Age seems to be the only available way to live a long time." Daniel-Francois-Esprit Auber (French composer)

"Those who believe strongly that death must come without physician assistance are free to follow that creed, be they doctors or patients. They are not free, however, to force their views, their religious convictions, or their philosophies on all the other members of democratic society, and to compel those whose values differ with theirs to die painful, protracted, and agonizing deaths." Justice Stephen Reinhardt. (American judge)

Chapter 14

If we come to grips with the meaning of life, and have reached a reasonable degree of contentment with our lives by our retirement years, then the terminational phase of our life can be—**BARRING BAD HEALTH**—a really relaxed and enjoyable period. We already have established that contentment must come from within, that others cannot give you contentment. Many an affluent parent has tried so hard to do that for their kids. You know, the worn-out—"I want them to have a better life than I". **WE MAY NOT HAVE TO EARN A LOT OF THINGS IN LIFE, BUT FOR CONTENTMENT WE DO. IF WE SEE CONTENTMENT IN OUR LIVES AS MAKING OURSELVES EVERYONE ELSE'S CUP OF TEA, CONTENTMENT WILL BE EVASIVE. IF IN OUR TERMINATIONAL YEARS WE SEE OURSELVES AS MAJOR PLAYERS IN THE GAME INSTEAD OF AS SPECTATORS IN THE BLEACHERS, LIFE IN OUR TERMINATIONAL YEARS IS GOING TO BE A BUMPY RIDE.** The people in the arena, in the productive stage of their lives, are not appreciative of someone in the bleachers pushing suggestions, voicing approval or disapproval of their every move. In the past all this was less of a big deal. I mean, you got old, had your heart attack, stroke, cancer,—whatever—and died shortly thereafter. The burden on others was of limited duration. Today, such a burden can be present for years, even decades, of attending to the elderly who have one foot in the grave and often are pretty much dead from the neck up. This is reality. The emotional cost of all this is tremendous—for everyone concerned—and the financial cost of it all even more tremendous. They say one third of medical expenses in life are incurred in the last years of one's life. The final days, these days, can go on almost interminably.

Being contented requires the ability to understand yourself, the nature of the evolutionary process, the relevance of the Golden Rule to your own state of mind, and being able to amuse yourself without needing others to be involved **SO MUCH OF** the time. If there is any stage in life when you need to self-generate your own amusement, your own interests, your own thoughts, etc., it is in the terminational years. In the formative years you BUILD, in the productive years you **PRODUCE**, in the terminational years you **REFLECT**, and have the time to do a zillion simple things you never had the time to do before. Once having achieved a degree of contentment in life, usually a long process, there is no need at all to twist yourself into a pretzel to please others or to be a nuisance to others, most of whom have their own lives to live, their own interests, their own agendas, their own likes and dislikes, etc. And this pertains to everyone in our lives—offspring, new friends, old friends, relatives, former co-workers, etc. Change is an operative word in the evolutionary process and change occurs in all of us, and relationships that once had so much meaning may have been altered in new times and new environments. **CLINGING TO THE PAST ALWAYS COMES WITH A TERRIBLE COST**—a lot of frustration, a lot of pain, a lot of resentment. The goal is to never lose sight of the wonderment of this experience called life, the amazing environment in which it occurs, and the brilliance of God's created evolutionary process.

I personally am not hung up on exactly what God is. Nor do I imagine God is exactly waiting for me to conceptually get His image right. I suppose it would be nice if God liked me better than others, if God favored me over others, and if God is there protecting me from those laws of evolution which involve chance, genes, and environment. What rational reason can anyone conceive which would make any of us more important than others in the eyes the the Creator? **SELF SERVING WISHES, WHICH END UP SUPERCEDING REALITY, END UP INTERFERING WITH OUR GOAL OF ACHIEVING GENUINE CONTENTMENT IN LIFE.** We either go with the flow, or we circle the wagons—wrap ourselves in inherited religious dogma, identify those different from ourselves (the heathens), raise a bible of some sort in one hand, a sword (literal or legal or verbal) in the other, and fight progressive change ad nauseam, swimming upstream for imagined 'promised lands' which seem to fade further and further away as the stream takes us with the evolutionary current—**–WHETHER WE LIKE IT OR NOT**. I wonder how many people end their lives asking, "God, why has thou forsaken me?" The basic problem is that we only want to play the game of life **IF WE CAN BE SPECIAL**. Life is more like being in gym class where the gym teacher puts players on a team randomly and each team just goes out and plays their role the best they can.

(16) Relevant Attestations:

"Resolve to be thyself: and know, that he
Who finds himself, loses his misery." Matthew Arnold (British poet and critic)

"We would rather be ruined than changed
We would rather die in our dread
Than climb the cross of the moment

And let our illusions die." Wystan Hugh Auden (British born American poet)

"A foolish consistency is the hobgoblin of little minds, adored by little statesmen and philosophers and divines. With consistency a great soul has simply nothing to do. He may as well concern himself with the shadow on the wall. Speak what you think now in hard words and tomorrow speak what tomorrow thinks in hard words again, though it contradict every thing you said to-day....'Ah, so you shall be sure to be misunderstood'—is it so bad then to be misunderstood? Pythagoras was misunderstood, and Socrates, and Jesus and Luther and Copernicus, and Galileo, and every pure and wise spirit that ever took flesh. To be great is to be misunderstood." Ralph Waldo Emerson (American poet, philosopher, minister)

"Sit down before a fact as a little child, be prepared to give up every preconceived notion. Follow humbly wherever and to whatever abysses nature leads, or you shall learn nothing." Thomas Henry Huxley (British Biologist, writer)

"The mind is its own place, and in itself
Can make a Heav'n of Hell, a Hell of Heav'n." John Milton (English poet)

"Self reliance grows by exercising it, as a muscle grows strong by its use. Dependence on others creates weakness, which in turn calls for more dependence—a vicious circle which brings failure." (unknown)

"Self-discipline without talent can often achieve astounding results, whereas talent without self discipline inevitably dooms itself to failure." Sydney Harris (Essayist and drama Critic)

"Don't compromise yourself. You're all you've got." Janis Joplin (American singer)

"Nothing can bring your peace but yourself. Nothing can bring you peace but the triumph of principles." Ralph Waldo Emerson (American essayist and poet)

"The greatest thing in the world is to know how to belong to oneself." Michel de Montaigne (French essayist)

"Associate with the noblest people you can find; read the best books; live with the mighty. But learn to be happy alone. Rely upon your own energies, and so not wait for, or depend on other people." Thomas Davidson (Scottish-American philosopher)

"She was looking for something I could never give her." Again his dark eyes bored into Julia's mind. "You have something of the same about you, young woman. Take my advice: Don't think you will find it in another person. You won't. It's not there. You must find it in yourself." Iain Pears (English historian, novelist and journalist)

Chapter 15

The influence of societal 'culture' on anyone's quest for contentment in life is clearly there, but to what extent is hard to pin point. It would be interesting, if one could know such a thing, to see whether the happiness index has varied much from age to age. How contented were the native Americans prior to the presence of Europeans on the scene? How contented were the Greeks back in the days of Aristotle compared to the Greeks of today? If the premises promulgated in this treatise have any validity then contentment in earlier days, like contentment today, is mostly an internal accomplishment, a state of mind achieved, not bestowed on us from without. STILL, there are circumstances in an environment, including societal culture, which have a bearing on achieving individual contentment. Genetics can be a plus or a negative, parents can be a plus or a negative, and certainly 'culture' can be a plus or a negative. As with all other aspects of life, there is no level playing field regarding societal culture.

Gandhi, Buddha, and Jesus were all critical of modernity, using the word in its largest context. All rejected the 'modernity' of their day and instead insisted such a culture made a meaningful life more difficult. According to all three, modernity was harmful to many individuals and caused them to lead their lives in ways that harmed others. Acting in ways which harm others is not compatible with the Golden Rule. All three emphasized that **GOVERNMENT SHOULD NOT BE IN THE BUSINESS OF ALLOWING SOME TO BENEFIT AT THE EXPENSE OF OTHERS**. Thus, those being governed, collectively, have the duty to force government to be just to all members of their society, and to undertake measures to help level the playing field for all citizens. Gandhi, Buddha, and Jesus would all endorse Mill's ideas on individual freedom and rights, but would **NEVER SUPPORT UNREGULATED CAPITALISM, OR CAPITALISM WITH NO LIMITS**. Inherent in the teachings of all three, and in the Golden Rule, is a deep sense of social justice and duty. **UNREGULATED CAPITALISM, WHICH EXPLOITS WORKERS, CONCENTRATES WEALTH IN THE HANDS OF A FEW, AND RESULTS IN THE EXPROPRIATION OF WEALTH FROM OTHER COUNTRIES, IS SIMPLY INCOMPATIBLE WITH JUSTICE AND THE GOLDEN RULE**. And here, in my view, is the important catch. All those who buy into, or support, such an unregulated capitalistic system, with no limits on the accumulation of wealth, have failed their ethical duties, and therefore limit their state of contentment. Remember, ethics implies there is a right and wrong, and a reward for right behavior. Otherwise, there is no purpose for ethical behavior. Every time we support a system which is unjust and ignores the plight of the less fortunate in order to amass excess wealth in the hands of ourselves or others, we have breached our ethical responsibility. Contentment, of any genuine sort, cannot be achieved in the absence of ethical responsibility. We know damn well most of our political priorities here and abroad for the past fifty years have been unethical. We know which side Jesus or Buddha or Gandhi or the other major religious prophets would stand with on all these issues. We really do know right from wrong—**THE ISSUE IS ALWAYS ONE OF WHETHER WE WILL DO, OR SUPPORT, THE RIGHT, AS EXPRESSED IN THE GOLDEN RULE,–OR SUPPORT WRONG FOR SELF- SERVING REASONS..**

The culture in which we live impacts our lives, and, as part of our environment, influences the ease or difficulty with which we achieve contentment in our lives. This is not to say, however, that we cannot find personal contentment in a nation ruled by democracy, or socialism, or communism, or a dictatorship, etc. We can find contentment in countries where the dominant religion differs from our own. Using the same logic, we can also find contentment whether we are tall or short, attractive, ugly, or plain, athletic or non-athletic, scholarly or non-scholarly, gay or straight, etc. The ease with which individual contentment can be achieved varies a lot and, in some cases, given the cards in hand, cannot be fully achieved. There are losers in the genetic component of God's evolutionary process–yet that does not mean the losers cannot achieve some level of personal contentment. For them to do this requires ethical behavior on the part of those with a genetic advantage. No matter our environment, personality, or diverse genetics, most of us can use our own reasoning to formulate logical beliefs and evolve ethically, via practice, until a degree of contentment can be reached in our lives. Can total contentment be reached? My inclination is to say no. For one thing I can't even define total contentment. As with all other aspects of living, the levels of contentment will be diverse and personally unique. Contentment is not an all or none phenomenon. It makes little sense to see diversity everywhere except in levels of contentment. **THE MEANING OF LIFE IS TO REACH A LEVEL OF CONTENTMENT–THE HIGHER THE BETTER.** Since achieving contentment is the personal meaning in our lives, the greater the degree of contentment the more successfully we have lived our lives. That our personal achievement is tied to the welfare of those less fortunate, via the Golden Rule, is precisely the means whereby God's evolutionary process has made available to the human species the possibility for a more level playing field and justice for all. I suppose it is like in a game where the players have the potential to work together–to strengthen the less skilled–and, through this teamwork, reach success for all. It would be useless for the individual players to pray for the coach to let them win the game. And it would be even more useless for the players to pray to God to let them win. **THE POSSIBILITY FOR PERSONAL CONTENTMENT IS THERE FOR HUMANITY, BUT NOT IN THE ABSENCE OF MEETING OUR ETHICAL RESPONSIBILITIES TO OTHERS VIA THE GOLDEN RULE. THERE IS NO SUCH THING as selfishly achieving contentment**. If we cannot stand diversity, and cannot share our excess good fortune with the less fortunate, we pay the price in the degree of contentment in our lives. It is in this sense that most prophets, including Gandhi, Buddha, Mohammed, and Jesus preached against the 'modernity' of every age. Materialism and personal gain are always present in every kind of human culture, but the lack of reward available from chasing 'modernity' as a means to a contented life simply proves 'all that glitters is not gold'.

American 'modernity' involves **MASSIVE MILITARY EXPENDITURES; MILITARY BASES ALL OVER THE WORLD (over 500); A VOLUNTEER ARMY OF 'MERCENARIES' (USING THE WORD IN A RESTRICTED SENSE); THE ACCUMULATION OF WEALTH IN THE HANDS OF A FEW; UNRESTRICTED CAPITALISM; UNRESTRICTED ACCUMULATION OF WEALTH; A 'FAMILY VALUES' CULTURE WHICH ENCOURAGES FAMILIES TO HOARD WEALTH, CIRCLE THE WAGONS, AND GATE THEMSELVES OFF FROM THE LESS FORTUNATE; FIGHTING WARS VIA**

DEBT ON THE NEXT GENERATION; VALUING PERSONAL LIBERTY MORE THAN PROTECTING THE HEALTH AND EDUCATION RIGHTS OF ALL**, etc. We have a **HUGE PLATE** of modernity to distract us from our most important goal—to achieve contentment in our lives.

As Buddha stressed, **WE HAVE A PERSONAL OBLIGATION, AS ADULTS, TO QUESTION EVERY SINGLE THING WE WERE TAUGHT AS CHILDREN**, to use reason as the means to evaluate every issue, and begin to practice ethics via the Golden Rule (Gandhi didn't use this term). **WITHOUT THIS EXAMINATION** we accept everything on modernity's plate and become trapped in this human devised rat race. We need learn not to talk about freedoms which, in reality, are freedoms for the few at the expense of the many. **ENCOURAGING UNMODERATED CONSUMERISM IS LIKE MOST EVERY GOOD THING IN LIFE–TOO MUCH OF IT CAN KILL YOU, IF NOT LITERALLY, THEN FIGURATIVELY, BY PLACING CONTENTMENT OUT OF REACH.** It has been my observation that some of the most contented people are those whose addiction to modernity is minimal; whose priorities in life are based more on simple pleasures, simple goals–an understanding that enough is as good as a feast; whose interpersonal relationships are diverse, non-judgmental; and whose generosity is directed to those most in need, not to relatives or anyone else not in such need. Part of 'modernity', a part that has been part of 'modernity' for a long time, is the idea that accumulated wealth should be passed on to offspring, not put back into society from which it came and specifically to those most in need. None of the prophets of any major religions preached selective compassion. **THE LEAST FORTUNATE HAVE ALWAYS BEEN THE FOCAL POINT OF EVERY ETHICAL MOVEMENT**, and just as surely these movements become polluted and trashed over time. What former prophet would recognize our **GLITTERING TEMPLES, OUR ORNATE RITUALS, OUR ROBED CLERGY, OUR TWISTED RELIGIOUS DOGMAS** as the essence of their ethical message? None of them. This is ethics twisted like a pretzel, run like a business, and as corrupt as the temples Jesus preached against. (It need be repeated again that **NOT EVERY** person associated with modern religion is corrupted by 'modernity'.)

At a younger age I considered the culture of Native Americans quite primitive, especially their religious beliefs. After all, they worshipped the sun, rocks, animals, etc. Everything to them seemed to have a spirit of some sort. Now I have come to see it in a more charitable light. Earlier I stated every gift must have a gift-giver, that the world we live in is a wonderful gift, and I viewed God as this gift giver. In this respect the American Indians were right: **EVERYTHING AB0UT THIS GIFT SHOULD BE CHERISHED AND APPRECIATED FOR THE IMPORTANCE OF ALL THESE COMPONENTS TO THE WHOLE–the whole being our universe. IN OUR CURRENT MIND SET, WHERE HUMAN ACHIEVEMENTS IN SCIENCE ARE GIVEN AN OVERRATED IMPORTANCE TO LIFE, WE ESSENTIALLY HAVE LOST RESPECT FOR OTHER SPECIES AND EVEN THE NATURAL RESOURCES OF OUR PLANET**. Some actually believe we have been given dominion over all other species and our natural resources. Whatever we need we just take; whatever species are a nuisance we chase into oblivion to varying degrees. This, to me, is simply madness—and invites 'Mother Nature' to come to bat, take the necessary swings, and make us pay the price for this self serving and ignorant attitude. Humans have overrun the whole planet; there are no more undiscovered continents to find and exploit. Just as we so often know the right and do the wrong, for all sorts of self serving reasons, we know the price any species must pay for overpopulation—anyone who ever had a high school course in Biology understands this. Yet, **WE**, writ large, refuse to let reason get in the way of our wants and emotions. **WE ARE SO DELUDED** that almost all believe it is okay for the earth's population to double again, as it has in my lifetime, and all will be well. It seems clear who is not all that well with their thinking.

The American Indians, in essence, should be included among those who agree modernity forces us to lead lives which alienate us from each other (outside immediate family), and from the world of nature we inhabit. From this perspective we adopt a regime of ideology and morality that dictates how we see the world, and as we do this, we end up leading lives that are ever so busy, but unreflective, self-serving, and meaningless. I no longer laugh at how the Indians saw everything around them as so sacred. Perhaps that is why I spend so much time out in nature, **ALONE**. It is not only good exercise but it constantly reminds me how 'sacred' all the components of this evolutionary process are; it helps me lose any tendency to see myself as anything more than a mere part of many special components. Commodity fetishism, and seeing things only in terms of economic value, distances us from the natural world, and sends us off scurrying along, en masse, like lemmings racing mindlessly toward the edge of a cliff. This mindless scurrying in no way leads to personal contentment. One misstep and we can get trampled–and if we keep on this mindless driving pell mell en masse far enough, we are over the cliff. We may already be in the start of a free-fall, some sort of evolutionary correction.

I like to think all of this musing so far is a reasonable use of logic. However, I cannot find any such reasonable logic to include the influence of love, sex, or children on the attainment of personal contentment. What may seem so obvious is never so with any of these topics. Part of the problem is the inability to make very many, if any, general statements about these important aspects of life. If anything is personal and all over the map, these three topics reign supreme. More than half of marriages don't seem a good fit; raising children seems at best a very risky lottery, sex is not only an illogical topic, but a drive which seems to have endless variations, all of which, given the variation, are fodder for more jokes than any other topic of human behavior. From a distance it all makes good theatre, but up close it not only reeks with emotional stress, but can cause divorce, career implosions, social isolation, and even imprisonment. This is where the ethical principle of the Golden Rule becomes inoperable. Really now, this 'do unto others as you would have them do unto you' hardly cements a good sexual relationship. Imagine trying to counsel two partners how they should act in bed. Maybe one enjoys oral sex and the other doesn't. Good luck with that. And the variations go on forever, both in types of sex acts and frequency. No wonder the feelings and laws about sex are a hopeless quagmire. Most of the time majority rules, but that has nothing to do with the rationality of anything. There may well be nothing better than a good marriage, while a bad marriage is tragedy, but really, there is nothing, it seems, worse than a bitter divorce. No marriage at all just produces a void to varying degrees. Everyone wants the perfect mate, but then everyone wants to be the best looking, the richest, the smartest, the most athletic, etc. **JUST WANTING, FOR SURE, IS NO PATH TO PERSONAL CONTENTMENT.**

The influence of marriage on contentment is present as a part of our environmental input. Nevertheless, since contentment comes from within based on the factors already belabored, even marriage, in itself, is no road to contentment. Many of us tend to view marriage as some sort of sacred, permanent relationship, and a coupling which, if terminated, is a sin. **YET**, if change is a major operative force in the evolutionary process, then on what basis are we to consider marriage exempt? All relationships change over time. To insist otherwise, in the case of marriage, is to be illogical, to swim upstream against the very nature of life itself. Some marriages last successfully over time despite the changes in the relationship, others do not, and some last in name only. Frankly, when we look at most couples we may often wonder what the hell cements such a relationship? When so many people fret so much over who should be allowed to marry whom, what is the logical reason for this concern? As with varied sexual acts, right cannot be determined by anyone's own personal feelings about a specific sex act. There are no facts to be sorted out here. There are people who might say "I can't stand broccoli", but that hardly is sufficient reason to make eating broccoli illegal.

Sound reasoning can only be made in the absence of emotion. If the logic of my treatise here on achieving personal contentment as the meaning of life is sound, then it is very possible for one partner in a marriage to achieve contentment and the other not. So what do we call that marriage–a good marriage or a bad marriage? Over time reason has led us to view marriage by less rigid standards. There is nothing sinful about ending a marriage, nothing sinful about living a marriage in name only, nothing sinful about remarrying. Of course children complicate the decision whether to stay married or not. Each circumstance is different. There certainly is plenty of evidence from enough studies to illustrate a single parent can be a very effective parent. Like many issues we tend to want the answer to be an all or none one. Either single parenthood is less effective or it is not. What is best for everyone involved is always a case by case answer. What we can assume logically is that **GOD DOES NOT BLESS OR SANCTIFY ANY MARRIAGE**. If He did, marriages would by definition last. The alternative is to insist God blesses marriages but He is not very perceptive and makes mistakes, I guess in this country half the time. We always want to involve God in our actions, probably as some sort of insurance policy. If we can't find a way to feel God is blessing our actions, then we begin to worry about getting that ticket to Heaven.

When we don't follow our human innate ethical nature, we always find a way to believe our behavior is a legitimate exception to the Golden Rule. **IF WE ARE SELF-SERVING, THEN FAMILY OR PERSONAL ADVANCEMENT TRUMPS OTHERS, AT LEAST NOW AND THEN, UNTIL THERE IS NO THEN**. Self-serving individuals expect God to take care of themselves and their families before others. No religious prophet ever said that, the Golden Rule doesn't say that, BUT our hearts tell us that the God we have created for ourselves certainly expects us to put ourselves, our families, and others in our own culture, country, or circle of friends before others. After all, we always seem to view God as having favorites—not among any other species of course, but just the human species. If that is not a self serving view of the evolutionary process, nothing is.

The best I can do with love, sex, marriage/children as they relate to personal contentment is to once again emphasize the importance of dealing with reality. Nothing about the evolutionary process is centered around us as individuals. We've covered that. This includes our needs or skills when it comes to love, sex, marriage, or children. We all know endless examples of terrible marriages, terrible love experiences, terrible children, terrible parents, and certainly repellant sexual practices. We may not be able to logically define what would be a repellant consensual sexual act, but we know one when we see it. And we all see things through a different set of lenses, with a different emotional makeup. Accepting reality is an important necessity for the attainment of personal contentment. If you are not the best athlete, you aren't. Go on from there. If you are not the most attractive person, you aren't. Go on from there—you are not going to win the heart of the prom King or Queen. If you are not a particularly social person, you aren't. Go on from there. If you are not the sharpest knife in the drawer, you aren't. **DON'T PURSUE A CAREER IN WHICH YOU ARE AT THE BOTTOM OF THE TOTEM POLE.**

If you can't accept the reality that **TOO MUCH OF ANYTHING IS BAD FOR YOU**, then the resulting addictions will close the path to contentment. **ADDICTIONS ARE EVERYWHERE**—from over eating, to over sexing, to over betting, to over watching TV, to overachieving at work, to over parenting, to overuse of recreational drugs, etc. Achieving contentment involves accepting moderation as a good thing. If we really take the time to understand ourselves, and use the best reason at our disposal, in the absence of emotions, in the absence of faith-based inherited dogmas, in the absence of indoctrinated social and cultural biases, then we have the best chance of achieving love, the best sexual partner, selecting the best spouse, appreciating the diversity of others, and being the best parent no matter the nature of any little ragamuffin under our care. **REALITY, REASON, HUMOR, AND ETHICS ARE THE NOTEWORTHY CHARACTERISTICS OF OUR SPECIES. IF WE CANNOT EXCEL IN THESE AREAS WE CANNOT ACHIEVE A CONTENTED LIFE.**

It is postulated here that if our human ethical nature is half assed, that is to say, typified mostly by some sort of passive sloppy sorriness for the less fortunate, this half-assed ethics is of no use as a means to attain personal contentment in our lives. Our ethics must be of an active nature for personal contentment to be achieved. What is active ethics? Active ethics is the application of the Golden Rule to your thoughts and actions. This is exceptionally simple conceptually. If people years ago had simply asked themselves whether they would have liked being required to sit in the back of the bus, the answer is evident enough, and their resistance to change unthinkable. Yet it took riots and killings before some people got permission to sit in the front of the bus, and only over the anger of the conservative right. We may start out life very conservative. But once we understand that change is a major operative component of God's evolutionary process, change is as natural and as to be expected as the sun rising in the morning. The trick is only siding with the **RIGHT KIND OF CHANGE**.

ACTIVE ETHICS CAN TAKE SEVERAL FORMS AT SEVERAL LEVELS. We can be fair and kind to all those with whom we come in contact. That is a good start. We can be actively involved with the less fortunate via work or efforts outside of our job; we can politically support those policies which support efforts to give the less fortunate legitimate help; we can share our own personal wealth, above the basics, to help level the playing field for the less fortunate; we can, at death, give the wealth we have accumulated to the least fortunate. Not a single one of these actions would be contrary to what every religious founding prophet, in probably every major religion, preached during their lives. We all know every one of these above ethical actions is admirable; everyone, everywhere, on the planet, not mentally challenged, knows **ALL OF THESE ACTIONS ARE ADMIRABLE—that is to say ethica**l.

The problem is we live in a world of competitiveness, a world in which we get caught up in self serving priorities. In simpler times there may have been far less materialistic conveniences, but there was far more time to personally think through the meaning of life and it was easier to see the forest for the sake of the trees. Today, we are inundated around the clock with propaganda as to what will make us contented. Little of it has any connection with ethics, with others, or with the nature of the evolutionary process. Almost all of it has to do with **THINGS**, the accumulation of more and more **THINGS**, and the **THINGS** can be material comforts, entertainment gadgets, titles, power, personal appearance, and anything else which can enrich us personally in some way. If democracy is failing before our eyes it is because politics has become mostly a pitch to personally benefit the materialistic lives of whomever constitutes a politician's personal base. In essence, the whole process is focused on just who is going to get the biggest piece of the common pie. **IT TAKES A LOT OF MONEY AND DISTORTION OF FACTS TO EFFECTIVELY IMPRINT A SELF SERVING BELIEF INTO THE MINDS OF OTHERS**. I think most people have become tired of being snookered or overwhelmed by the complexity of modern problems, and they thence just shut it all out. When Jay Leno meets with the man on the street to ask questions, we see so clearly how much reality many people have just shut out of their minds, and that their lives obviously have become a small world of immediate personal whims and satisfactions. They feel personally toyed with by life, much as a cat might toy with a mouse before the kill. Their world becomes reduced to a handful of close friends or family with whom they babble unimportant trivialities and momentary emotions via electronic gadgetry their entire waking hours. There is little substance to their lives, no expansive thoughts, no practiced development of their powers to reason, no practiced development of their ethical potential. These people have zero chance of ever becoming contented with their lives. **MODERNITY HAS WON**. Every religious prophet has warned against this happening.

I want to repeat what becomes the crux of the matter for all of us. "Active ethics can take several forms at several levels. We can be fair and kind to all those with whom we come in contact. That is a good start. We can be actively involved with the less fortunate via work or efforts outside of our job; we can politically support those policies which support efforts to give the less fortunate legitimate help; we can share our own personal wealth, above the basics needed to live a good life, with the least fortunate; we can, at death, give the wealth we have accumulated to the least fortunate." **WHAT WE CAN AND WHAT WE DO** do are quite separate. No one did anything but admire Andrew Carnegie, one of the richest men in the world, when he gave all his acquired wealth away. No one really harped away that he should have given all this acquired money to his children. No one. No one claimed, including his children, that he was not a good father. **NO ONE CRITICIZES THE PERSON WHO LIVES A MODEST LIFE, SAVES A LOT OF MONEY, AND THEN LEAVES THE MONEY TO CHARITY**. No one. We all know these are all ethical actions. However, we also have individuals close to us that we love dearly (offspring, other relatives, certain friends, etc) and we prefer to give them an inheritance over the less fortunate who, for the most part, we don't even know. In American culture we have got the notion that to give our wealth, upon death, to the less fortunate somehow means we like our own offspring less. This is silly. If we collectively cannot help those less fortunate with our excess wealth, we cannot save those who are well enough off, and we certainly are not following the Golden Rule. We need always remember that God gave us, collectively, the ability to help the less fortunate by always striving to make the playing field more level, and it is simply self-serving to imply that, through our prayers, it is God's responsibility to help the less fortunate, not us because we want to help our own offspring, friends, etc. Our own children are certainly special, every one of them. Likewise all God's children are special—every one of them, to God—and for anyone to claim their own children take precedence in the larger scheme of God's evolutionary process, is simply illogical.

After all, none of this implies any less care or attention to our own children, friends, etc. than we already give. It simply means our excess wealth goes to the less fortunate, to give them a more level playing field. Besides, we in America like to brag that it is most admirable to make our own living, our own accumulation of wealth. Finally, we have already postulated that contentment comes from within, and that means we can't give contentment to others via inheritance. No, to do the right thing, the ethical thing, is to give our excess wealth in a way which makes the playing field for the less fortunate more level, or helps protect our environment, or improve health care for those without it, etc. We can do both, we can love and nourish our own children to death and also be ethical in the distribution of our excess wealth. Were humanity, collectively, to follow the Golden Rule and give our excess wealth to the less fortunate–if we collectively did this–then there would be no people starving to death, dying from curable diseases, homeless, without proper medical care, etc. Many of us prefer to pray for, rather than act to share our own wealth with, the less fortunate.

It could be construed here that I am asking parents to put the less fortunate before their own children. **THE KEY WORD HERE IS CHILDREN**. The obligation of every parent to their own children is of paramount importance. How to be the best parent to a child is among the most difficult and greatest challenges humans face. Every parent is different, every child is different and the best parenting style for one child may not be the best for another child. The environment for parenting differs, the economic status of families differ, the health status of parents and children differ. How to be the best parent is beyond the scope of this musing and beyond the experience or knowledge base of my own life. The point in question here, at this point in this musing, about gaining contentment in our lives, is how to ethically live our lives given that contentment cannot be achieved with unethical actions. When children become adults parental responsibility is transferred and adult offspring are then responsible for their own lives. It has nothing to do with altering affection for offspring. What organized religion (not the original prophets), culture, and materialism have done is to make the unethical appear to be ethical. We have already established that it is unreasonable to view ourselves as more important in the evolutionary picture than we are. If we ourselves are not the focus of divine protection of some sort, then it becomes a bit illogical to think our own kids are in reality any more important than anyone else's kids in this evolutionary process. Because our culture, religions, and the pursuit of the almighty dollar have warped our sense of ethics we end up approving the sharing of our wealth, not to the less fortunate, but to our offspring, relatives, or friends. Parents now feel trapped; it is expected of them to give their excess wealth to their kids or other relatives when they die and even while alive. And if they do not, their kids will be insulted and angry. One of your adult kids might actually end up in life being one of the least fortunate in life and then, and only then, do they qualify as the ethical recipient of your excess wealth. **IN A HEALTHY SOCIETY CHILDREN, WHEN THEY BECOME ADULTS, ARE SUPPOSED TO EARN THEIR OWN WAY THROUGH LIFE, THEY ARE SUPPOSED TO BE RESPONSIBLE FOR THEIR OWN SUCCESSES, THEY ARE SUPPOSED TO START OFF WITH LESS AND GRADUALLY EARN THEIR WAY TO AFFORD MORE.** And of course, once they too have earned enough to have excess wealth past the basics, they are ethically required to share any excess with the least fortunate. How many families are driven apart over time as the offspring jockey for position to inherit parental wealth? In a healthy society offspring would not even expect, in the absence of being among the least fortunate, to receive an inheritance.

THE BEST INHERITANCE ANY CHILD CAN RECEIVE IS TO HAVE BEEN THE RECIPIENT OF GOOD PARENTING. After that they are, by nature of being adults, on their own. Only those who seriously believe there is no ethical obligation for humans, collectively, to make the playing field for all God's people more level, can justify using their own wealth to adjust the playing field for only their own children. It would be a like a judge who states there are separate laws for their own kids and a different set of laws for other people's kids.

Relevant Attestations:

"The best inheritance a parent can give his children is a few minutes of his time each day." Orlando Battista (Canadian-American chemist and author.)

"There are only two lasting bequests we can hope to give our children. One of these is roots; the other wings." Hodding Carter (American journalist and author)

"I would as soon leave my son a curse as the almighty dollar." Andrew Carnegie (Scottish-American Industrialist)

Chapter 16

Ethics requires moderation in our chase after the almighty dollar. Let there be no hedging here. For many Americans it is really the almighty dollar which competes with our innate ethical potential. 'Enough is as good as a feast' may be an ideal mental state, but it takes some effort and patience to adhere to this crucial point. One can debate honestly enough just what constitutes enough. Like is it a house with 1,000 sq. ft., 1500 sq. ft., 2000 sq ft., 4000 sq. ft, etc. Americans have always viewed capitalism as a wonderful system. Of course capitalism does not have to be an all or none proposition. Capitalism is a good system IF it is not unregulated and IF there are limits set. The same is true with putting strict personal limits on what constitutes enough wealth or how much one can spend on a particular item like a car or a house. The solution is not that difficult. Once we have gained a decent income from our job we need to practice active ethics. That is to say **WE NEED FOREVER REMIND OURSELVES THAT OTHERS COUNT AS MUCH AS WE DO**. So, to enforce this ethical principle we need to spend as much on others as we do on ourselves when we have excess wealth past our basic needs. **IT IS NOT BEING STATED HERE THAT NO ONE CAN BUY AN EXPENSIVE CAR OR EXPENSIVE HOUSE, ETC**. If you can afford to buy a $50,000 car as opposed to a $20,000 car that is fine **PROVIDING** you match the $30,000 extra expense with $30,000 on those less fortunate. If you only have $30,000 extra to spend, then you compromise and you buy a $35,000 car and give $15,000 to charity. Somebody else may wish to spend that extra $15,000 on a house or whatever. Perhaps one feels they need save a nest egg in case they have expensive medical costs at some point. Fair enough; then the excess money can be distributed upon death to the less fortunate.

Most parents find this abominable. Their charity with any excess money is going to go to their kids. The bond between most parents and their kids is correctly and expectedly strong. The problem is one of what constitutes parental responsibility. The responsibility of parents to properly care for and nurture their children is self-evident. Every religious prophet, and every logical thought process, reinforces parental responsibility toward their offspring. To say otherwise would be to say we have an equal responsibility towards all pets, not just our own. This, of course, would be silly. The difference is that pets are dependents for life. We cannot say, "OK, pet, you are four years old—an adult—out the door you go". With children it is totally different. Here the object is to raise children in such a way that once they mature they can go out on their own—**FOR THEIR OWN GOOD**.

Earlier in this treatise it was stated that the best reasoning is done in the absence of emotion. The emotional bond between child and parent is extremely strong. A good parent wants to do everything they can for their child. But at the same time, there comes a time when the child is grown, and, in the absence of unusual circumstances, the child, for the child's own sake (certainly including giving them the right to achieve contentment in their lives), requires that the child become his/her own unique being and 'dare to think' on their own, to question everything their parents or any others have ever taught them, and to achieve successes in their life **ON THEIR OWN**. This is the real evolutionary nature of new generations of most, or all, species. To cripple a child for life via overprotective parenting and self serving fawning over an adult offspring seems more self serving to the need of a parent than any real need of the offspring. There is an old saying, "Give me a fish and I eat for a day; teach me to fish and I eat for a lifetime". My own dad used to tell his kids that once reaching 18 years of age we were on our own financially. And he meant it.

From a practical standpoint, the principle that our accumulated wealth, upon death, is going to the less fortunate should be established early on and often. This goes a long way in heading off any anger at the time of our death. Current American culture has offspring expecting to get parental wealth upon parental death. To do otherwise would be interpreted as some sort of hostility to their offspring. I suppose if a parent dies while the offspring are still kids the ethics changes here. But in most cases the offspring are not kids, but independent adults not in the least fortunate category. The ethics involved in God's evolutionary process is not focused on any individual trees, but on the whole forest. In the big picture, evolution is an amazing, progressive, awesome process. The process aptly fits the phrase "no pain, no gain". That is to say, diversity and change are crucial aspects of the process. No diversity, no change. No change, no progress. For humans, unlike other species, the ability to comprehend pain, including its consequences, is highly developed. Thus, for humans to limit the pain for those less fortunate requires collective ethics to enable the less fortunate to live more comfortably and with more contentment. We cannot be ethical with the notion, 'screw the less fortunate—we are taking care of ourselves and our own family'.

ORGANIZED RELIGION AND COMMON CULTURE HAS BASTARDIZED THE ESSENCE OF ETHICS WHICH IS KNOWN THROUGHOUT THIS TREATISE AS THE GOLDEN RULE. For a parent today to give their acquired wealth at death to the least fortunate is easily interpreted as disrespect for their own offspring. Of course it is not. And in a truly ethical society, which has its head on straight regarding ethics, children would not expect, in the absence of themselves being among the least fortunate, to receive inherited money from their parents. A truly ethical society, which has its head on straight regarding ethics, would not expect to treat excess wealth in a manner which does not consider others just important as themselves. It is illogical to pretend it is someone else, God or whoever, who makes life so unfair, who makes the playing field so un-level. We are always asking God to make it more level, to show mercy to the less fortunate and yet God has given the human species the ability, through collective action, to make the playing field more level for more people. **"WE HAVE MET THE ENEMY AND IT IS US WHO ALLOW SO MUCH UNFAIRNESS TO EXIST IN THIS WORLD"—NOT THE REFUSAL OF THE CREATOR TO MAKE IT ALL RIGHT.**

If everyone followed the Golden Rule in their actions and thoughts, there would be no homeless, there would be no refugee camps, there would be no people lacking proper health care, there would be no children attending poor schools, there would be no problem of more and more wealth accumulating in the hands of a few in any society, no matter the form of government. Heredity, chance, diversity, and environment will always create different levels of achievement in any area of human activity. Competition is not wrong—it is the engine which drives God's evolutionary process. **CAPITALISM IS NOT WRONG; BUT UNREGULATED CAPITALISM WITH NO LIMITS IS WRONG.**

My dad told both my brother and me that when we were 18 we were on our own. Through his actions toward us when we were growing up there was never any doubt of his support and love for us as his children. Because we fully expected to be on our own after adolescence, his statement wasn't considered an act of disloyalty or loss of love or anything of that sort. If children didn't expect themselves to be the recipient of parental accumulated wealth at death, there would be no negative feelings about it, there would not be the typical hard feelings about who got what and how much. If we had not learned to accept "it is my money and I will spend it all on myself if I want", then we would not do so knowing the real consequences of adopting this attitude—namely, the inability to ever really be contented with our lives. The requirements for personal contentment in life are basically to use our own ability to reason as the path to formulate our own goals and priorities in life, to make a good effort to reach our inborn potentials in any area, to know ourselves well enough to know our own strengths and weaknesses, to appreciate and support diversity among humans, and to **ACTIVELY** practice the Golden Rule so that we really do unto others as we would have them do unto us—this meaning **ALL OTHERS**, not just our own family members or friends or fellow countrymen or carbon images of ourselves in any other way. There is nothing in the Golden Rule, when the Golden Rule itself is culturally accepted as the basis of ethics, which will weaken the bonds between parents and offspring, the bonds between friends, etc. Adult offspring who would be offended by their parents giving their accumulated wealth upon their death to the less fortunate are no ethical persons themselves. Inherited wealth is not earned wealth. After all, we like to say everyone should earn their own way. That often gets distorted to mean it is okay for the fortunate amongst us to faithfully wait in line to be given mom and pop's accumulated wealth. Of course this runs against the grain of the Golden Rule, the 'real' American way, and fairness.

This must be made clear: the less fortunate who receive help from the more fortunate in life are not going to be made contented by this act of generosity. Money spent on the less fortunate, to be effective, just makes the playing field more level. After that, these less fortunate, like everyone else must then make their own success in life and achieve contentment the same way as everyone else, via living the Golden Rule.

Since having myself adopted the practice of spending no more on myself, past the basics of living, than I do on the less fortunate, I have achieved a more contented life—more contentment than ever before. If I die and am able to leave all my money to the less fortunate, and that could include any family members in that category, then in my mind, the right thing has been done. Period. I am surrounded by people who have enough money and then some to have the basics needed to live well. Why, for any reason would I wish to give them gifts or agree to accept any gifts from them? This is frivolous social silliness. Any friendship based on exchanging gifts between individuals who are in no need of gifts is simply misplaced ethics. Gift-giving, in terms of material stuff and money, should always be between the haves and the have-nots. I guess if this need to give materialistic presents to friends is important to us, and we take this money from the half of the excess we spend on ourselves, then it is okay. It is at least honest; we are doing it for ourselves, our own needs—in this case the need to exchange gifts.

A relationship between a person's job and personal contentment exists but the extent of the relationship is hard to decipher and probably varies from person to person. The best that can be done here is to make some general observations. It is probably important that we all seek a job compatible with our personal strengths and weaknesses. Again, realism need drive our career goals. You might badly want to be a singer, but if you can't sing, you can't sing. And so it goes. Furthermore, in general it is not best to select a field of work in which you will be on the bottom of the totem pole ability-wise. This is asking to be kicked around, vulnerable to the least job security, deflated confidence, diminished job satisfaction, and limited promotional opportunities.

WE NEED SELECT OUR BOSS WITH CARE. There are, in general, two kinds of bosses—those who demand everything be done their way and are adamant about that, and those whose simply want employees to get the job done well and are less concerned about variations in ways to achieve a goal. And there are, in general, two kinds of employees—those who are content to do it the boss's way, and those who are content only if they can do their job in a way which fits their own manner of doing things. To get the right mix we sometimes need switch jobs, just to get a different kind of boss.

The autocratic kind of bosses are the least likely to be contented with their lives. Spending a lot of time trying to force square pegs into round holes is not exactly conducive to generating personal contentment. Furthermore, this does not meet the spirit of the Golden Rule. Each of us would like to get whatever the job needed to be done, done our own way. I suppose, if our job is to connect a part to a car on an assembly line there is no room for variation. But many jobs are not so cut and dried. In this case any rules that exist need be directly related to facilitating getting a job done well. **THE BEST BOSSES ARE THE ONES WHO SEE THEMSELVES THERE TO ASSIST EVERY EMPLOYEE TO BE THE BEST AT WHAT THEY ARE**

BEING ASKED TO DO, PERIOD. For example, I suppose a boss might have a personal preference as to hair style. But hair style has nothing really to do with job performance, certainly not in almost all cases. **BUT,** one might argue, some customers might not like a certain hairstyle. Herein lies the crux of ethics. **MAKING OTHERS DO THINGS SIMPLY TO MEET THE PREJUDICES OF OTHERS IS UNETHICAL.** Thus, we just don't do that, and to the extent we do, it just makes it that much harder for us to live a contented life. Remember, a contented life is very much dependent on developing our ethical potential. This takes both practice and commitment. To go through life hedging here and there is simply unethical and limits personal contentment. **A HEALTHY SOCIETY IS NOT PROMOTED BY HONORING THE PREJUDICES OF SOME AT THE EXPENSE OF OTHERS.** The object is to demonstrate an appreciation of diversity so that the appreciation of diversity becomes a social norm. **MAJORITY RULE IS NEVER A LEGITIMATE DETERMINATION OF ETHICS.**

All of the above dictates that **RULES SHOULD NEVER BE FIXED IN STONE**. Sometimes a rule does not help generate its intended purpose. To say there can never be any exceptions to a rule is to deny the existence of diversity among a population. There is this common perception that to exempt anyone, on a case by case basis, from a rule is unfair to those who are made to follow the rule in question. This is simply not true and demeans the intelligence of others. For example, there might be a rule that states if you miss more than 3 classes, in the absence of documented ill health, that you are dropped from a class. The rule is there because it helps generate a higher passing rate for the course. Nice rule. But if the fourth absence is because the person had a flat tire en route to class, where is the justice to drop the student from class? The solution is simple, the reasons for abrogating a rule in the interest of justice is simply made public to all those governed by the rule. The real challenge is to make the rule a better rule. For example, where I once taught, the institutional rule was that after three missed classes a student was to be dropped from the class. I amended the rule for my classes to read that if a student was not passing the course and missed three classes they would be dropped. The object is to pass the course. If someone can pass the exams via means other than coming to class, well so be it. I may be disappointed that I didn't play an important role in their passing, but they did pass and to pretend otherwise is unethical. If someone can learn something without much help from me what does that have to do with how much they learned?

Effective ethics is not sloppy sorriness nor allowing others to order us to be unethical. "I was just doing as I was told" is unethical. Every one of us who supported the Vietnam War or participated in it, committed senseless murder of two million Vietnamese. **BLIND RELIGIOUS OR PATRIOTIC FERVOR NEVER TRUMPS ETHICS**. In the much milder case illustrated in the former paragraph, the solution was simple. The university rule trumps my own classroom rule. I suppose it does. However, I simply told the administration I will pass such a student and if the administration orders me in writing, signed by the appropriate administrator, I will withdraw the passing grade. In that way, I did the 'right' thing, and some other specific person over me did the 'wrong' thing. The point here is that **WE ARE ALWAYS REQUIRED TO BE ETHICAL TO THE EXTENT WE HAVE THE POWER TO BE ETHICAL**. The draft dodgers in the Vietnam War could not by their actions stop the War, but they did permit themselves a high degree of contentment in that they did the ethical thing. They cannot be blamed for the needless slaughter of two million Vietnamese.

Convenient ethics, ethics interpreted as majority rules, ethics imposed by others above us, is wrong. **WHENEVER WHAT WE DO DOES NOT MEET THE TEST OF THE GOLDEN RULE WE ARE WRONG.** It is that simple. We all are wrong, probably way too often, some more than others, and thus, the degree of individual contentment varies too. Personal contentment is not an all or none proposition. We cannot separate into two groups, the contented and non- contented. There is not a thing written in this musing which is etched in stone as some sort of eternal truth. But whatever is written erroneously or sloppily can only be corrected by better and more logical reasoning. When the world was figured out to be round, this observation could not be refuted by simply saying, "Well, I believe very strongly that the world is flat." When someone says "I strongly believe", we can be pretty sure they also mean reason is not a thought process which is about to change their belief. Certainly when someone tells us "God says so", that is the ultimate dismissal of reason. It tells us two things: first, are any of us really in a position to refute what "God says", and secondly, how special and important must this person be who purports to have been personally instructed by God? If someone kills another person claiming that "God told me to kill them" we dismiss them as mentally disturbed, but if another person tells us "God is against abortion" this is supposed to be accepted as the ultimate final irrefutable conclusion on the issue.

I suppose having spent so much time using the word contentment in this musing I ought to precisely define the term. For a period of time it seemed to me that it was just the word 'pornography' which was impossible to define. What is pornographic to some is simply not pornographic to others. 'Contentment' is probably another word which cannot be precisely defined, another one of those 'I can't define it but I know it when I feel it'. **CONTENTMENT IS A STATE OF MIND THAT MOSTLY COMES WITH AGE, IF EVER.** Of course when we are young we are full of wants. We want to be popular, we want to be good looking, we want to be a good athlete, we want to be a good student, we want to get into a good college, we want to do well in college, we want to graduate and get a good job, or not go to college and get a good job, we want to have intense and many sexual orgasms, we want to meet and marry the best spouse in the world, we want to have the best house in the best part of the world, etc. The list of wants is endless. Some of it we are programmed to want, like an expensive sports car.

Like a popular song tells us, there is a time to be born, a time to die, a time to grow, etc. Life is ever changing and changing times bring changes in our wants, our understandings, our feelings about a lot of things. With all this change around us, it is difficult not to feel often that the rug is being pulled out from under us. It is. Only if we understand the nature of the evolutionary process can we roll with the punches and not end up all discombobulated, irritated, and unhappy. What we learn early on in life is to be realistic about our wants. We may want the best looking spouse with the most charming personality but we are not likely a candidate to be in the running to get that; we may want to be a star athlete on a team but most likely we are not in the running to be that; we may want to be the smartest student in school but we are not likely to be that either. Hell, it is no surprise many people just give up. It seems to them all that they want is out of their reach. The mission for all of us is to try and be satisfied with what we have or what we are capable of achieving. To do this one needs to accept the reality of God's evolutionary process, and to understand THINGS cannot bring contentment. For example, we might need a car to get from place A to place B in a comfortable manner. Most every car has comfortable seats. For us to get from place A to place B in a Prius is just as comfortable as getting there in a Cadillac. All the other stuff is just programmed needless wanting. The problem is we have a strong desire to be entertained every moment of the day. Of course we need entertainment of this or that sort BUT to fail to develop the ability to entertain ourselves with our own thoughts, plans, ideas, and appreciation of diversity in life, is to deprive ourselves of the chance to be contented. Contentment comes from within; no one can make us contented. **No THING** can make us contented. **AND WHAT WE WILL BE MOST CONTENTED ABOUT ARE THE THINGS THAT ARE THE PRODUCT OF OUR OWN THINKING, OUR OWN ACHIEVEMENTS, OUR OWN INDEPENDENCE, AND OUR OWN DEVELOPED ETHICAL BEHAVIOR.** Everything is always two-sided. There is ourselves and there are others. Until the balance between the two is equal no real contentment in life can be achieved.

RECREATIONAL DRUG ABUSE IS A REFLECTION OF DISCONTENTMENT. It represents nothing more than an attempt to alter your mental state in an artificial quick fix way. Compulsive behavior should never be confused with contentment. More to the point, addictions reflect lack of contentment. A contented person is not motivated to find solace in an array of addictions. People can get addicted to a wide array of behaviors from overeating, sexual compulsive behavior, gambling, seeking attention from others, work, sports, TV, traveling, recreational drug abuse, shopping, etc. Almost by definition addictions are an attempt to find some sort of contentment in our lives. **NO FORM OF ADDICTION, INCLUDING RECREATIONAL DRUG ABUSE, SHOULD EVER BE TREATED AS CRIMINAL ACTIVITY.** Spending vast millions of dollars on making addictions a criminal offense and jailing the victims is not only a waste of money, but simply pushes the victim further away from achieving any degree of contentment. When Barry Goldwater stated "moderation in the pursuit of justice is no virtue" he may not have meant it in the way I will use it here. Justice, in the context of reaching a degree of contentedness, involves practicing the Golden Rule. That is to say, whenever we ourselves count more than others, justice—ethical justice—is not done. It is easy enough to see too much of our lives through our own lenses, our own needs, our own material needs, our own happiness, our own beliefs, etc. It should always be 'here is what I want and this is what the least fortunate need'.

(18) Relevant Attestations:

"I often compulsively pursue happiness no matter how bad it makes me feel" Unknown

"Cocaine isn't habit forming. I should know - I've been using it for years." Tallulah Bankhead (American actress)

"Just cause you got the monkey off your back doesn't mean the circus has left town." George Carlin (American comedian)

"The chains of habit are generally too small to be felt until they are too strong to be broken ." Samuel Johnson (English author)

"The time will come when humans can do almost everything with the technology and still one thing remains impossible, releasing addiction on technology." Toba Beta (Indonesian author)

"Sexual addiction is the fastest growing addiction in the United States. It's based in part on the fact that obtaining sexual literature, pornography, is so convenient today. It's more readily available. It is there at the click of a finger." David Bird (British bridge writer)

Chapter 17

Contentment is not the absence of anger, the absence of wanting, the absence of stress, sadness, etc. A contented person has the whole array of normal human emotions. A contented person is not going through all the hours of the day singing "zippidy-dee-do-dah-day". So what then is contentment? Contentment comes from the genuine appreciation for the chance of being alive, and for having the chance to improve ourselves, and being truly thankful for whatever good luck has come our way, including the many people who enabled some good luck to come our way. **BUT IT IS ALWAYS A TWO-WAY STREET.** To go through life like a sponge, soaking up all the help from others, becoming too impressed with our own accomplishments, and failing to share our good luck with the less fortunate will prevent us from ever being contented. The ethical nature of humans is of a social kind, it is never a one sided equation. It is never about just us, or our family, or our circle of friends, or our local community, or our own country. There is no ethical prophet who ever existed who has ever pretended this to be so. **CONTENTMENT IS NOT ABOUT 'FAMILY VALUES'; IT IS ABOUT HUMAN VALUES AND THE EXTENT TO WHICH WE SHARE EXCESS PERSONAL WEALTH, POWER, FAME, AND**

ACHIEVEMENTS WITH OTHERS ON AN EQUAL BASIS. It boils down to so much for me and an equal amount for the less fortunate.

We may well be on our way to some kind of cataclysmic evolutionary event due to human overpopulation of our planet, but Mother Nature always bats last, corrections take place, and if it takes a hundred thousand years to recover, evolution continues on. **NO LIVING SPECIES YET HAS EVER BEEN THE END POINT OF THE EVOLUTIONARY PROCESS.** In my own time I have seen progress in human rights and myriad new ways to elevate human standard of living for some. It has truly been, for some, the best of all possible worlds and, for others, as our population density increases exponentially, the worst of all possible worlds. Our materialistic talents currently have outpaced our ethical development. But we can probably rest assured that ethical progress in God's evolutionary process will catch up, through the Golden Rule, after the shit has hit the fan, and human ethical behavior eventually will ensure all people have a home, land to live on, a job with a living wage, access to good health care, schools which are of good quality for all children, and so on.

When we spend an inordinate amount of energy and time focused on our own needs and wants in life, any gains are of a peculiar personal nature. The rewards are often there and forthcoming, but to get the same feeling of pleasure over time requires bigger results. It easily becomes a roller coaster ride with every high followed by a bigger depression which requires a more intense effort for whatever the addiction is, to get an adequate high. **PLEASURE SHOULD NEVER BE CONFUSED WITH COMPULSIVE BEHAVIOR.** We can plant electrodes in the so called 'pleasure centers' of the brain, attach the other end of the electrode to a bar which, when pressed, stimulates the 'pleasure center' and the animal will press that bar all day, neglecting to even eat, etc. It is simply irrational to say the animal is experiencing pleasure, let alone any contentment. It is really almost the opposite of contentment. Much of our own behavior is of the same unrewarding nature. There are people who feel compelled to wash their hands a hundred times a day. This is compulsive behavior, not pleasure, and certainly not contentment. I suppose, in some sense, **ONE OF THE REWARDS OF REACHING A RELATIVELY CONTENTED STATE IS THAT WE LOSE COMPULSIVE BEHAVIORS**. Contentment can be viewed as "Heaven on Earth". Even if it turns out there really is some sort of after-life Heaven, finding a way to reach a contented state on earth is no small reward.

CONTENTEDNESS SHOULD NOT BE CONFUSED WITH HAPPINESS. Everyone experiences happiness of some sort at certain times. Your team wins, you get a promotion, you have sex with someone of interest, you recover from an illness, you get the expected high from a recreational drug, etc. Obviously, everyone who has had these kinds of happy feelings is not a contented person. Remember, contentment comes from within, not something anyone else can give to you, or any drug can give to you. Parents may try oh so hard to give us contentment, a spouse may try oh so hard, friends may try oh so hard, employers may try oh so hard, etc. That does not mean any of these 'others' cannot influence your ability to become contented. Conversely, a contented person is not immune from sadness, from frustration, from disappointment, and from properly directed anger. What contented people seem to have in common is independence, a healthy sense of humor, tolerance to diversity (empathy with all sorts of people), an absence of revenge, a dedication to justice for all, and moderation as a trait of life. Contented people do stand out. Lincoln, for example is a good example of a very contented person. Of course he was sad during the Civil War, of course he was frustrated, etc. He would have been abnormal not to have been. But he had all the signs of personal contentment—independence from others, a healthy sense of humor, a tolerance to diversity, endless empathy with others, a dedication to justice for all, and moderation as a trademark of his lifestyle.

I doubt anyone would seriously consider Rush Limbaugh a contented person, to use an example of someone highly discontented. His sense of humor is to trash others different from himself; he has no empathy for diversity, no interest in justice for all; he has an addiction to drugs, to notoriety; he seeks contentment through a pursuit of money, along with a strong sense of revenge towards all sorts of people. Pat Robertson, Sarah Palin, Barry Bonds, Michele Bachmann, Adolf Hitler, Donald Trump–these are examples of highly discontented individuals. This list could be expanded almost forever. So can the list of contented people, and most of them would be entirely unknown. Barack Obama is clearly a contented person, Mother Teresa would fit, Dwight Eisenhower would, Billy Graham would, Hank Aaron would, Andrew Carnegie would. In terms of wealth, fame, and power there is an army of people with little of any of these who are quite contented in life. Again, contentment comes from within, the illusionary gems of 'modernity' in any age cannot create a contented state. That is not to say all the wealthy or famous or powerful are never contented. It was never alleged in this treatise that a wealthy or famous or powerful person cannot be contented. It has been postulated that wealth, fame, or power are not the stepping stones to contentedness. Everyone would like to be physically attractive. Some are, but who is attractive has nothing to do with wealth, fame, or power. Contentedness is of the same nature.

Chapter 18

Creationists have this view of the world as something created by God, much like humans assemble an automobile. And of course humans are His favorites and certain humans are God's personal favorites, at least to the extent they follow God's word and dogmas via inherited religion. This is called pure faith-based religious belief. **THESE BELIEFS WERE NOT ARRIVED AT VIA REASON BY THE BELIEVER BUT VIA INHERITANCE AND WORDS WRITTEN BY ANOTHER HUMAN DECADES AFTER THE PROPHET IN QUESTION HAD DIED**. There is no logical evidence to support this as any means to be in contact with God, and mountains of evidence exist to dispute such beliefs. The existence of prophets of various sorts can be established, and they may in many cases have been ethical leaders, but being a connection to God is quite another thing. If everything said in this treatise were true and based on reason (neither totally likely), it in no way means it represents any message from God. Rather, it is just reasoned that God created the evolutionary process and this process is governed by God's laws of evolution. If one creates the game of poker one is not responsible for who wins or loses at this game. No one is forced to play poker. No one is forced to live in the evolutionary process. We were given existence by chance, dealt a particular genetic and environmental deck, and simply given an opportunity to achieve some personal contentment in our brief life. No one can judge when another person has had enough of life, for whatever their reasons. Creationists see it differently. To them life is sacred no matter what (at least in theory, but never in practice). For them, only God decides when enough is enough. Unless, of course, there is some modern medicine or medical operation or procedure which will snatch death right out of the hands of God. The more Creationists are pushed, the more irrational becomes their defense of their beliefs. It is so obvious that their beliefs are based on pure faith, that if one attempts to discuss their beliefs rationally, almost all of them will say, "I don't want to talk about it". If pushed, they contend they are right because they have been 'saved', that God communicates directly with them, and we are only ignorant because we have not been 'saved'. That is their ultimate safety valve. Now who could possibly contest that? If God talks to them and not to us, the question then becomes, "Is God right or are others?" Of course by definition God is always right. What is not clear is whose perception of God is correct, and on what basis do some humans think God is communicating directly with them.

If the scientific knowledge gained about the evolutionary process is faulty, then everything in this treatise is suspect. If the scientific knowledge gained about the universe is faulty, then of course the earth may still be flat. If my interpretation of all the statements by major religious prophets is wrong, then of course there is nothing wrong with amassing great wealth and not sharing it with the least fortunate. When Jesus said it would be easier for a camel to pass through the eye of a needle than for a rich man to enter the Kingdom of Heaven, either our understanding of language is imperfect or Jesus never said it, or most Christians simply choose to skip over such unsettling statements. When the Bible says if a human has sex with an animal the animal must be killed, or any other such amazing statement, either the Bible is wrong, or our ability to reason such things out is defective. If the Bible is only right some of the time then how could it possibly represent the Word of God? Does this mean God only knows what He is talking about some of the time? I guess once we are 'saved' our personal communication directly with God gives us the inside scoop on these matters. What kind of God would go around giving 'inside scoop' to select individuals via inherited religious dogma? It isn't reason which gives us such notions, but rather a self serving need to create a God who fits comfortably in with our own personal behaviors. Mobsters going to church every day is the ultimate example of such illogical behavior.

If the process of evolution is taken seriously, then clearly the living forms of life are ALL imperfect. If not, then the evolutionary process is over. It would be hard to envision on what basis we might think the process of evolution is over. If this process is not over and will continue at some point without us, as annoying as that might be to us, then while we live we will be confronted with all the imperfections in existence. All of us will be subjected to injustices, small and large, of one sort or another, as long as we are alive. We have stated that part of achieving a contented life is to always side with everything which promotes more justice for everyone—the Golden Rule. Thus, it is obligatory for us to be for justice in all matters as best we can. But the other side of the coin is how we ourselves react to injustices against our own personage. Again, our responses need be based on reason, impacted by our emotions as little as possible. If basic emotions are allowed to rule the day then our lives become an endless pursuit of revenge. Does anyone seriously think we can live a contented life if we never forget and we never forgive? Obviously every scenario is different.

Most matters are best forgotten and we move on with our lives. On what basis can we expect endless perfection in a world filled with imperfections? The neat thing about the evolutionary process is that these imperfections become self corrected over time. One of the reasons the United States does not rank high up the ladder on countries which have the highest contentedness index is that we have bought into a massive **THINGS** industry and an obsession with **LAW SUITS**. If there is no such thing as a mistake, all that is left is a crime. When there is a crime the guilty, and the guilty alone, should pay. As a corollary, others—those beside the victim, should not become wealthy as a consequence of someone else's misfortune. Remember, we cannot become contented by someone else making us contented. A child dies, let's say here, because of criminally negligent actions on the part of a doctor. We'll avoid here what constitutes criminal negligence. The doctor should pay the price, whether it be monetary or loss of his medical license or jail. There is zero reason why the surviving members of the family should receive thousands or millions of dollars as a settlement. "Wait," someone will say, "These people need to be compensated for their grief". Really? If the child had died of natural causes is there not tremendous grief also? Should every parent who loses a child be given thousands or millions of dollars? Certainly, by the Golden Rule, if one deserves it, the others do also. Two sets of parents are faced with the death of a young child they cherish dearly. One set of parents gets a million dollars and the other set of parents get zip. The logic is ludicrous on its own standing, but also remember—money cannot bring contentment. So on what basis are we taking public monies from somewhere to give to only some bereaved people and not others?

The acknowledgement of the Golden Rule as the essence of an inherent human ethical trait is not only universal but the basis for ethical decisions. It is hard to do wrong following the Golden

Rule. Perhaps there is this constant contest between 'modernity', used in every historical context, and ethics (the Golden Rule). We can worship 'modernity' or the Golden Rule. Notice I used the word 'worship'. Modernity does not have to be rejected, just not used as an endpoint to contentment. Our giving excess wealth to the least fortunate does not cause us to forfeit our ability to be content (from the loss of that wealth). Just the opposite—contentment cannot be achieved in the absence of ethical behavior. There is never a one-or- the-other situation between 'modernity' and ethical behavior. Some religions have tried to imply this—that to possess some modern devices is to be sinful. The trouble is, as with all addictions, more is not necessarily better. Actually, too much of almost anything can kill us—including food, oxygen, work, etc. Excess is an interesting word and its meaning almost dictates restraint. When we say capitalism is good, that doesn't necessarily mean it is good unrestrained. When we take a recreational drug to give us an occasional high, that doesn't mean it is good to take a drug to escape the obligations and realities of our lives. Watching a movie provides pleasant escape from a daily life, but watching movies to replace getting a life is a problem.

Understanding the Golden Rule, our genetically built in compass for moral behavior, as the path to personal contentment, is no complex process. Look at all the moral dilemmas in history. Would one wish to be forced to ride in the back of a bus? Of course not, so supporting such a law is unethical. Lincoln said, "As I would not wish to be a slave myself, I would not wish it on another." "If slavery is good," Lincoln went on, "then it is a strange good in that it is is not a good for everyone." The Golden Rule can be applied in most every instance of social behavior. Do we wish ourselves to select whom we marry? If so, then why would we wish to deny others the same freedom? Gay marriage is a no-brainer. Opponents would say, "Wait a minute, homosexuality is an aberrant of nature—a sexual aberration." Not so since homosexuality in other species is not uncommon at all. As for sexual aberration, good luck with defining that one. Is any sexual act which does not result in fertilization unethical? There goes kissing, flirting, masturbation, every kind of sexual fetish, and sex when one partner is infertile. If we wish to have the right to pursue our own sexual activities in bed, then of course others are free to pursue consensual sexual activities of their own choosing. What is so difficult about the Golden Rule? And why shouldn't those who are the best practitioners of the Golden Rule be the most contented in life? Furthermore, the Golden Rule is available to every person everywhere, regardless of financial, religious, ethnic, social status, or any other category we might employ to divide up humanity. Anyone can be ethical. But not everyone can achieve contentment. Certain genetic and environmental circumstances, in the extreme, can effectively shut down contentment. **BUT**, and this must be written large, **BUT**—the Golden Rule, practiced by enough others, can level the playing field to enable a huge number of humans to achieve contentment who otherwise could not. For example, why is it necessary for any human to die of a curable disease? Why is it necessary for anyone willing to work to be unable to find work? Are there no tasks to be done which will make this a better world to live in? Why should so many wallow in wealth while so many wallow in abject poverty? The Golden Rule, as practiced universally, would absolutely not allow such injustices to prevail.

Pray as we might, and often do, the reality seems to be that so much of what we pray for we already have the power, collectively, to provide some relief to those for whom we pray. Then there are the kind of prayers in which we pray that someone will beat cancer, or a stroke, etc. Now really, on what basis are we to expect God to selectively protect individuals from death? First of all, God's evolutionary process demands birth and death as part of the process, just like it demands chance and diversity for evolutionary progress. The evolutionary process has worked fine for millions of years and it worked well before we arrived and it will work well after we are gone. We ought to really quit trying to make ourselves more important than the process, or be some kind of special 'being' in the process. There is certainly nothing wrong with our being delighted at the chance given for life, and the opportunity to achieve some contentment in the process of living.

Lower animals cannot comprehend the significance of suffering, which is to say they have no higher sense of inherent ethical nature or death. But humans do, an evolutionary improvement, and this enables humans to prevent suffering, to help the least fortunate, and in the process achieve personal contentment. **HUMANS, COLLECTIVELY, HAVE THE MEANS TO LIMIT SUFFERING, TO ENABLE JUSTICE TO PREVAIL, TO LEVEL THE PLAYING FIELD FOR THE LESS FORTUNATE.**

The term contentment, as used in this treatise, needs to be more precisely defined. It is not a temporary emotion such as anger, happiness, sadness, etc. These emotions are temporary states of mind we all have from time to time. If the intensity, duration, or frequency of these emotions gets too far off, this constitutes a medical condition requiring treatment of some sort. These emotions are mostly generated by the effect of others or the environment on ourselves. Contentment, on the other hand, is generated from within. A contented person is fully capable of emitting anger, sadness, and the whole range of human emotions. **CONTENTEDNESS IS CERTAINLY NOT AN ENDLESS 'ZIP-A-DEE DO DAH DAY' STATE BY ANY MEANS**. A contented state frees us from the pettiness of human interactions.

There are no axes to grind because we have come to understand human nature, our place in the evolutionary process, and we have accepted our ethical responsibility to the Golden Rule.

Abraham Lincoln is an example of a contented person. "Wait", some would say, "he was stressed out to the maximum, had a life seeped in tragedy, and had periods of intense sadness." Yes, he was under tremendous stress. He did not choose all this stress, but it came his way. But again, contentment is not something that comes from without. Without all the stress dumped in his lap Lincoln would still have been a contented man. With it, he was still a contented man. Few in history have been as effective as Lincoln when it came to the Golden Rule. The key word here is effective. Remember, real ethics is an active ethics, not robotic rituals, not blind obedience to sectarian dogmas, not something applied whenever convenient, not something that is inoperative if we cannot by ourselves bring about justice. There were plenty of people who were more outspoken and decisive on the ethical issues of the Civil War era than Lincoln. But they lacked the brilliance of Lincoln to effectuate change. Because of his inner contentment, Lincoln was able to be as strong as a steel cable, bending this way and that way as the wind blew, but ever so surely he brought the nation to the point of destiny desired—just like a steel cable may bend with the wind but it gets to its point of destination. **NO ONE HAD A BETTER TAKE ON LIFE OR FELT MORE COMFORTABLE WITH HIS OWN 'SELF' THAN LINCOLN.**

This is not to say contented persons always succeed in bringing more justice to others. They don't always succeed. BUT, their actions are in the right direction. As noted, ethics without action is no ethics at all. At the very best it is disingenuous ethics. We all know people who talk the talk, and yet practice the Golden Rule selectively. That is not real ethics. That is self-deception, self-serving, self-fawning, self-delusional scheming. Often they have a bible of some sort in one hand, a patriotic flag in the other, support every war, and wrap themselves in some form of 'family' values. The family can be self; self and spouse; self, spouse, and children; an ethnic group; a religious group; a cultural group; etc. There is often this mindless faith-based allegiance to some sort of special group. It is never logically clear why any particular group of humans is so special. Is the human species the only species within which God has favored groups? One thing is for sure: these intolerant-to-diversity people are not contented people. They rant, rave, ridicule, and condemn endlessly, often from a pulpit surrounded by glittering grandiloquency, buried in endless rituals. It is the height of huftymagufty unethical blather. The effect, intended or not, is to make the unethical feel ethical. Organized religions often provide subtle shelter, housing self-denial of unethical behavior as a kind of pablum for those seeped in self-serving 'modernity'. It is not ethics, but Things or Titles or Power which drive their lives. Again, it is not wrong to seek things, titles, power per se. All of these can become effective **TOOLS** to maximally effectuate the Golden Rule, thereby maximizing personal contentment in our lives.

Chapter 19

An understanding of God's created evolutionary process, coupled with a practiced adherence to the Golden Rule (the human inherent basis for ethics) and a consistent use of reason as the basis for behavior and thoughts, enables us to understand the idiocy of "I achieved my success the old fashioned way—I earned it". People who put themselves front and center on this "I earned it" bit, are simply using this charade to dismiss their obligations to the Golden Rule. The implication often is that "if I can do it so can you, and if you choose not to, so be it—tough luck".

By any reasonable logic, my own life has been reasonably successful, if I can use the term loosely. I caught just about every childhood disease prevalent in my environment, but fortunately there were treatments available to prevent me from dying. Born a hundred years earlier I would have died in childhood. Luck. I was born into a supportive responsible family. Luck. I was born into a safe, working class neighborhood. Luck. I was enrolled in decent schools. Luck. I had playmates who were good influences on me. Luck. I inherited the ability to run at a good pace for a long time. Luck. I'll stop here; the point is already made. Of course we ourselves have to play the cards dealt, but it is grossly disingenuous to place ourselves as the singular and most important determinant of our success. Luck, genetics, environment, and the help of others via the Golden Rule play a huge part.

Suppose I didn't have any luck at all in the areas above. Then I would need assistance to achieve any successes in life. That is the essential and foremost function of innate human ethics. The purpose of ethics has less to do with ourselves and everything to do with others. Any form of life with a minimal nervous system can innately act to protect itself. Self serving human actions performed to the detriment of others, or with indifference to the welfare of others, are unethical and the consequences of such unethical behavior, in varying degrees, prevent us from achieving much personal contentment.

SO, what are the characteristics of personal contentment? **INDEPENDENCE IS ONE.** Since contentment comes from within there is not this endless need for others to make our day satisfactory. **APPRECIATION OF DIVERSITY IS ANOTHER.** There is no need for everyone to be a carbon copy of ourselves, and appreciation of diversity provides endless fodder for entertainment and understanding while broadening our perspective on the amazing diversity of human life. Contentment stimulates our curiosity as to what makes others tick, matching our curiosity as to our own peculiar personality. Contentment means we have learned that 'enough is as good as a feast"; those for whom enough is never enough live tortured unfulfilled lives. Contentment means not sweating the 'small stuff' in life. In the end, given the nature and magnanimity of God's evolutionary process, it is almost all small stuff. People who are contented are not frightened to death of death. For the most part, people who are contented can be trusted. Since the Golden Rule governs their actions, contented people are not going to stab others in the back, stiff others in dealings with them, or mistreat others who are different from themselves. Contented people are not people who use 'family values' to wall themselves and their immediate families off from society, circle the wagons, and operate as if life is one big US versus **THEM**. Contented people radiate a genuineness about themselves, there are not a lot of forced smiles along with meaningless insincere compliments, while pretensions are absent or minimally present. Contented people tend to stand out and be well- known in their neighborhoods, work places, etc. That does not mean they are necessarily leaders of anything. Perhaps it can be put this way: ethical behavior implies a duty; this duty implies a reward; the reward is contentment right here on earth irrespective of whether there is any life after death.

On the other hand, contentment does not imply a person is immune from misfortune. This is clearly not one of the rewards for ethical behavior. There is no God who is going to drop a protective shield around us for ethical behavior, protecting us from health catastrophes, injustice from others, financial woes, accidents, etc. The very best of us can suffer from the worst of catastrophes. If history has shown anything, it has shown this to be true. Of course this never stops millions of people from worshipping a God they believe will do just that—protect them from all the land mines of life. In reality, their beliefs become the basis for varied unethical behaviors. An extreme example of this are mafia characters who go to mass every day. It seems a good number of people who go to church a lot go precisely because they think this will gain them forgiveness for their unethical actions which permeate the rest of their lives. Even more amazing, many of these people genuinely weep over the misfortune of others across the globe and yet continue to hoard wealth and procure more wealth over the backs of others. The Golden Rule is simply an inoperative mode of their life outside of token miniscule contributions to a church, contributions which primarily go to support the vast cost of glittering temples and church employees.

The real meaning of life—to maximize the degree of contentment in our lives—will not be achieved by amassing a small army of friends who look like us, think like us, feel like us, act like us, have a personality like us, live like us, etc. More to the point, this sort of restricted limits of reality ensures a level of fear, resentment, and general intolerance towards diverse others, a resentment which is incompatible with contentment. We cannot appreciate what we do not know, do not understand, do not experience, and is outside our own realm of reality. It is not uncommon for it to be said that, "You cannot understand because you are not one of us". This is way overstated. For this to be literally true we could not understand anyone except ourselves. No one else is one of us. It is hard to be contented if we do not understand diversity. Isolation from diversity is like placing braces on our brains, a walled-off life that instills fear of others. a distrust of others, a dislike of others. Given the right circumstances, we are then vulnerable to release pent up emotions upon these perceived others in the cruelest of ways including mass killings, a genocidal crusade to get these misfits off the planet or at the very least out of our general vicinity. No one ever describes people loose with such released anger as contented. One of the easiest paths to placing blame is to blame societal problems—local, national, or global—on minorities of some sort or another, those amongst us who fail to meet minimal requirements of our own self-images. We know who they are—they dress differently, they have a different skin tone, they are of a different religion, they talk differently, they resist knowing their place, and in general they generate in ourselves a feeling of discomfort about them.

It is easy enough to sense when someone doesn't really like us. They may make every effort to be 'politically correct' in their verbal communication with us (I prefer the term morally correct) but there are enough non-verbal vibes to enable us to see through the verbal correctness. When I was teaching, I observed that those teachers who had little respect for some students, for whatever their perceptions of them, had no luck hiding their real feelings, no matter how hard they tried to camouflage their feelings with verbal correctness. It is often not understood that little contentment is generated by appreciation of those most like ourselves. This is, of course to be expected. Rather, a far greater degree of contentment is achieved by successful interrelationships with those different from ourselves. A genuine act of kindness to others different from ourselves usually elicits a response of gratitude that is uplifting to the giver of the kindness. In my own teaching career it was not uncommon for a student different from myself, let's say black as an example, to look puzzled at some point and say something like "I didn't know it was possible to talk to a white person about things this way". Every time we break through the barriers of diversity we have lived up to the Golden Rule big time, and the reward, in terms of contentment, always follows. It is like we finally understand diversity is a major player in God's laws of evolution.

God is not about us as individuals, God is about the whole spectrum of life and planetary resources. If we cannot accept this, then contentment levels in our lives will always be limited. It is like we are saying to God, "Look, if I can't be special, and entitled to special favors, and be exempt from some of your evolutionary laws, and be assured of a heaven after death, life for me cannot be contented." And it won't if those are our terms. Too many people seek contentment via special relationships with God and end up all discombobulated, emotionally feeling at some point,

"Why have You (God) failed me?" When we see terrible things happen to the best of us we often are aghast that God **LET** this happen to them. The answer of course is that God is not about **US** or **THEM** but about the process of evolution itself. Considering the whole process of evolution, having existed millions of years now and still going strong, God is to be admired; we all are lucky that by chance, a particular sperm met a particular egg, and we each then had the opportunity to participate in this phenomenon called life.

While the use of the Golden Rule as the basis for human ethical behavior may be simple and straightforward, still it serves to provide a basis for ethical behavior in myriad situations. Sexual behavior between adults is taken out of the realm of specific sex acts, and placed on the basis of a consensual relationship. If two people are sexually aroused and satisfied by a foot fetish, then so be it. If they enjoy hanging from a chandelier engaging in anal sex so be it. I purposely here tried to use extreme or ridiculous examples just to show there is no need for any strict limitations. After all, even in these two extreme cases, where is the unethical behavior? It affects no one else if they are both adults. Children are, of course, off limits considering their formative stage in life. What actually determines our eventual sexual inclinations is mostly not understood. Most people do not engage in particular sex acts because some pervert in a raincoat dragged them behind the bushes. When most anyone is asked why they like to engage in a particular sex act, even they themselves have no good answer, any more than any of us can answer how often we want sex. Maybe those with the lowest sex drives are the luckiest.

Aside from sexual behavior, all sorts of discriminatory actions are easily resolved by the Golden Rule. We want to choose whom we marry. Of course we do. Then so should every adult have that right. Period. We want our children to have access to good health care. So does every parent, and on what ethical basis should any child be deprived of that? We want our own children to be enrolled in good schools with good teachers. So does every parent and why should any child be deprived of that? If we are in need of help from the more fortunate in life would we want them to share their excess wealth to help us? Of course we would. And this leads us to an important reality of the Golden Rule: **OTHERS COUNT AS MUCH AS OURSELVES**. This is the whole basis of human ethics according to the Golden Rule. Does that mean some cannot, via their efforts and talents, be better off financially than others? No it does not. Every person has a personal obligation to provide themselves with the basics in life—adequate shelter, good health care, a way to earn a living, etc. But once all this is achieved, any further expenditure of money for ourselves should be matched by an equal expenditure of money for the least fortunate. What could be more ethical and simple?

In reality, a good percentage of the most fortunate in society actually see themselves as more worthy than others, and entitled to spend their good fortune any way they so choose. Perhaps they are entitled to do this, in the sense there is no law against it, nor should there be any such law. BUT, this kind of unethical behavior will never lead to any substantial contentment. Anyone who has spent any time around wealthy people knows exactly what is being stated here. It is no real surprise that the abuse of recreational drugs, gambling, divorce, shopping obsessions, traveling obsessions, and a host of other over-indulgences are especially prevalent in those who wallow in wealth, especially—but not exclusively—with those who acquired wealth via inheritance, unusual physical or intellectual talents, or stiffing everyone with whom they have come in contact. One of the most remarkable comments often heard in these times, when 2 - 5% of the people own 80 - 90% of the wealth in the United States, is the complaint that the wealthy pay something like 30 or 40 percent of the taxes while something like 30 or 40% of citizens pay no taxes. And people who bring up the 30-40% who pay no taxes are angry about it. Actually, some of those who pay no taxes are in the upper economic bracket, and the rest make so little money from their jobs that they are not required to pay taxes. And of course some would like to work but can't find a job. Then there are those who find a job which pays barely more than unemployment, so working a hard job to be poor when one can be just as poor not working so hard is not exactly a brainless decision. But not to worry. If we keep downsizing, reducing benefits, eliminating pensions, etc., the percentage of people receiving too little income to pay any income tax will go up. In the long run the Golden Rule is necessary to ensure a sustainable society. Most every empire of every sort in history has imploded **PRECISELY BECAUSE** the wealth became too concentrated in the hands of too few. Americans can act on this or insist we are going to be the first exception in history to avoid such implosion.

Chapter 20

If, by the Golden Rule, others count as much as ourselves, just who are the others? Can we target our grown children or other relatives to be the 'others'? Ethics dictates the answer is no unless these grown children or other relatives are among those people with the greatest needs. I can think of no prophet in any major religion, including Jesus, who ever identified adult offspring or relatives as targets to receive gifts of wealth. It is always those most in need to whom such excess wealth is directed. The 'American Way' has always put an emphasis on personal responsibility and the need to earn our own way in life. Psychologists have long recognized that, in general, the healthiest mental state is achieved by earning our own financial wealth. Most all parents naturally feel a strong bond to their own offspring and emotionally want to direct any excess money to such offspring. Yet, we all know that **WHAT WE EMOTIONALLY WANT TO DO IS NOT ALWAYS THE RIGHT ETHICAL COURSE OF ACTION.** This narrowed and irrational view of who the needy really are in society has created an unfortunate climate in which children view parents as obligated to provide financial support for them when they are adults, and certainly, at the very least, bound to leave their assets to them when their parents die. This is not what the Golden Rule implies at all, and in reality, this widespread practice actually implies that, for some self-serving reason on our part, we believe God sees our own offspring as more important than the offspring of others. Clearly this is myopic self serving nonsense. Upon what basis are we to believe God views our own offspring or relatives to be the 'least fortunate' in the ethical mantra, 'do unto others as you would have them do unto you'? The whole basis of ethics dictates that we ourselves are not more important than others, let alone our own offspring or relatives be more important than others. Until children are grown, parents do have a tremendous responsibility to their own children. An affection towards them will most often last a lifetime. Nothing wrong with that. Remember, however, the purpose of innate human ethics is to make the playing field more level for the less fortunate, to enable the less fortunate to have a better life despite the bad cards dealt to them by genetics and environment. We cannot, because of our emotional attachment to our own kids or relatives, act otherwise. More family members end up estranged from each other over inheritance and other financial distribution matters than any other reason. If people, in general, properly understood ethics and conveyed it repeatedly to their kids, the kids would never expect, as adults, to be the recipient of parental excess wealth. If they didn't expect it, there would be no noses out of joint over inheritance matters. There would be more peace and good will between siblings.

Contentment is stage-of-life dependent. The formative years, for example, are not conducive to any serious level of contentment. During these years we are all in the learning mode and emotions play the major role. Thus, we at different times are happy or unhappy, excited or bored, jealous or affectionate, etc. There is little yet to be contented about. If we have athletic skills, success here will bring happiness and peer recognition, which make us happier than otherwise. If we have academic skills, they will bring us happiness when we earn good grades. If we have good looks we may earn social successes which make us happy. The less fortunate, having been dealt few such good cards, will have to struggle more to be happy. Much of what follows in our later years is dependent on these formative years. Fortunately, happiness in the formative years is less materialistic than in the productive or terminational years. So, many of us, regardless of our economic status in the formative years, will look back upon them as happy times or unhappy times. Because our emotions play a more important role in our formative years, these are the times when we tend to reach our highest emotional peaks. As we grow older reaching such strong emotional peaks is far less likely.

At a certain level of wealth it becomes easier to generate even more wealth at a more rapid rate. And such wealthy individuals expect their happiness level to soar accordingly. But it rarely does. For one thing, there are more and more matters to keep tabs on to protect and manage the increasing wealth, whatever the nature of the wealth. So the wealthy find themselves in some sort of obsessive addiction. More, more, more doesn't translate into more and more contentment. Divorces, drug abuse, crankiness are rampant among the wealthy. And all this wealth requires attention to protect this wealth from others. Even friendships are suspect, constantly fueled by the desire of others to have some of the wealth trickle down on them. While strangers compete for access to some of the wealth, the offspring compete just as fiercely to ensure they get their 'fair' share of this wealth. Of course 'fair share' is actually nothing. Ethics and the 'American Way', at least in theory, demand that all of us earn our own wealth. While we are ethically bound to help the least fortunate on our globe, this doesn't mean we are ethically bound to make them wealthy. In most cases, absent a condition which places a child in the handicapped category, the best parents makes sure their children understand that after their formative years they will truly be on their own. It is really hard to develop any real degree of contentment if we do not earn our successes ourselves. Remember, contentment comes from within; no one can give contentment to us. Others can make the playing field more level for us, and they are ethically bound to do so via the Golden Rule, but given a more level playing field **WE** have to **RUN WITH THE BALL OURSELVES**.

The productive years are more concentrated on running well with the ball. Because the evolutionary process is based on diversity and chance, there is no prescribed way to run with the ball, or even which goal posts to aim for. What we do have in our productive years is a lot of energy, a lot of goals, a lot of opportunities, a lot of pressures (economic and social), and endless uncertainties. Our struggles during this stage of life can generate varying degrees of contentment. But again, the contentment arises because WE did it, not because **SOMEONE ELSE** did something for us. We cannot fool ourselves, if someone dies and leaves us a fortune of some worth, we can use that money for transient bouts of pleasure, but these are just transient emotions. We cannot fool ourselves into seriously thinking 'we earned all this', and no one else is fooled either. The ethical nature of the human species is such that unless the wealth is shared with the least fortunate, which is to say others count **AS MUCH AS** ourselves, there can be no real contentment. This cannot be repeated enough: the reward for ethical behavior is personal contentment. If there is a hereafter so be it. If there is not, then ethical behavior is not without reward, for such benefit is attained right here in our lives now. To be selfish is natural, we all have obligations to ourselves; but at the same time we have an **EQUAL** obligation to the less fortunate. The word equal here is a key word.

This equal obligation is not just in terms of money and material matters. Our politics need reflect this equal concern for others. It need be remembered that God's created evolutionary process is about diversity and change—never about equality or individual preciousness. This timeless process has evolved over millions of years and ethics is one of the evolved characteristics of humans. In most other species it is a more simple survival of the fittest. The evolved ethics has complicated all of this in that ethics is based on the Golden Rule. Others count. Others count as much as any of us. Like every other evolved characteristic, ethics is still evolving. Humans today overall are more ethical, in the broadest sense, than humans were thousands of years ago. The appearance of ethics in the evolutionary process creates unusual dilemmas. The invention of various religions in which there is a God who places individual demands on us, who expects us to worship Him in a specific way, and rewards allegiance to Him with special rewards and protections runs contrary to our inherent ethical nature. We want so much to be special, to be God's favorite, that we invent a God tailored to our personal needs. This ends up running almost contrary to the real essence of ethics. Ethics provides the basis for a better world for everyone, a way to be responsible inhabitants of the planet. Clearly there are kinks, serious kinks, yet to be worked out through the process of evolution. Because of human inadequacies with ethics at this stage in evolution **THE SHIT IS ABOUT TO HIT THE FAN**, so it seems, at least in my own perception of matters.

Of course humans must reproduce, and of course our offspring need an adequate environment within which to spend their formative years. We all know this. The problem seems to be that the transition from formative years to productive years is as difficult for parents as for the offspring. There is nothing in the Golden Rule which implies our own offspring are more important than anyone else's offspring. This does not mean we may not value them more, love them more, or be heavily concerned about their progress and welfare. Still, God does not put them ahead of anyone else, or provide them with special protections any more than God puts any of us at the head of any line or provides us personally with special protections. Now if God doesn't, who then does? The answer is found in the Golden Rule. **WE ALL DO**, or at least are ethically bound to do so. Thus, correct politics are never about us getting special perks, considerations, protections etc. Correct politics are always about collectively enforcing the Golden Rule, about leveling the playing field as much as we can for the greatest number we can. Current political issues are ripe with the need to adhere to the Golden Rule. The idea that we have an obligation only to take care of our own needs and the needs of our own family before the needs of others is not only unethical but puerile and self-destructive. Forget the self-serving notion that God favors this or that nation. History has shown this to be false. If Jews, for example, are really the chosen people of God, let's just all hope God doesn't switch and favor our own group. Come on now, if Jews are God's chosen people would He have let the Holocaust happen? That is really a stretch.

But let us put aside this question of whether God has certain favorite human groups. We could quibble about this, and it would shed no light on our current national and global problems. Consider this: if the Golden Rule prevailed no one would be dying of curable disease, no one would be without land to live on, no one would be without a job with a living wage, no one would be persecuted for their religious beliefs, no child would be without proper health care, no child would have less money spent to educate him than other children, no mentally disturbed person would be left to wander the streets in a mental fog, and there would be no such thing as unlimited, unregulated capitalism.

Given the dire consequences of human overpopulation to other species, and to humans themselves, there need be mandatory responsible reproduction. Yes, all of this is possible, and I would guess will someday be reality, notwithstanding the possibility of dire correction intervals in the evolutionary time scale before this happens. **THE ONLY CERTAINTY SEEMS TO BE THAT THE HUMAN SPECIES, LIKE EVERY OTHER SPECIES, WILL PAY FOR OVERPOPULATING OUR ENVIRONMENT**. So far, humans choose to have blinders on to this problem.

Contentment does not mean we need tolerate all kinds of diversity. Meanness, greed, or intolerance toward gender, ethnicity, religion, sex orientation, culture, economic status, etc. are legitimate targets for personal disapproval and anger. Contented people can be against a lot of things, can be angry about things, can become saddened by external events and display the whole array of human emotions. But in the midst of all the turmoil surrounding them, a contented person finds refuge in his/her adherence to the Golden Rule. There is solace in knowing that we are not the cause of the pain so many suffer, that our politics is centered around the Golden Rule, that any surplus of our wealth past the basics is shared equally with others less fortunate, that diversity is appreciated, not persecuted. I always use Lincoln as an example of a contented person. While he lived in tumultuous times, and had huge pressures on his Presidency, he kept his calm, his wits, his sense of humor, his sense of fairness—BECAUSE he lived an ethical life. If Lincoln didn't maximally apply the Golden Rule to his own life, no one has.

NONE SEEM TO FEAR DEATH MORE THAN SECTARIAN RELIGIOUS EXTREMISTS. There are exceptions. A few can't wait to strap a bomb to themselves and go to heaven by taking perceived heathens on a trip to hell as they ascend to heaven.

They, at least, truly believe God is deeply attached to them personally and has definitely saved a place in Heaven for them. But most religious extremists of inherited religions talk the talk, but seem scared to death of death. It almost seems like part of their psyche knows full well they have been picking and choosing which parts of scripture to follow, and know full well their lives and achieved wealth have hardly been shared equally with the less fortunate. It is hard to imagine that most Christians aren't at least vaguely aware Christ Himself would never support some politics these Christians support, or some of their behavior, or lack of behavior towards others. This internal conflict makes death a very scary proposition. Maybe they fear they are really going to go to Hell for some of their actions in life. It always seem strange, when I hear these fired up religious nuts spew forth their hatred of others different from themselves, that these religious purists sound so opposite to the words of the founding prophets of their religion—like Jesus for example. They certainly don't seem remotely like what Jesus preached himself—**NOT IN SUBSTANCE, NOT IN TONE, NOT IN ACTIONS, NOT IN THE WAY THEY LIVE.**

Contented people in their terminational years have little fear of death. Death is as natural a part of life as birth. Contented people are simply grateful they had at least a chance to be a part of the evolutionary process. Contented people aren't bitter because some others had better cards in their hands from the get go, or had better luck, or got more help from others. Contented people, one way or another, have come to grips with the nature of God's created evolutionary process, and learned to go with the flow, holding fast to the Golden Rule and finding comfort from all those they helped along the way, or those who helped them—the greatest comfort coming from helping those with the greatest needs.

It seems a lot of discontentment arises from our inability to deal with reality. **CONTENTMENT SEEMS TO REQUIRE ACCEPTING REALITIES AND MAKING A CONCERTED EFFORT TO BECOME AN UNDERSTANDING PART OF THE EVOLUTIONARY PROCESS.** Of course the level of understanding will vary, or at least the nature of it, BUT the search for meaning in life can hardly be successful pretending we are something we are not, that we have a special connection with God, that our emotions, unchecked, can lead to any kind of nirvana. If this were true we could let a child just go with his emotions as a means to achieving contentment. Such spoiled kids rarely, if ever, grow to contented adults. Diversity is never so evident as part of the evolutionary process as it is in varied human endeavors. There is no 'best' way to be a parent, to teach a subject matter, to have a romantic affair, to be good boss, to be a good employee, to be a good coach, to be a good teammate, to be a best friend, to achieve sexual orgasms, to live long, etc. A methodology one person may find successful another may find unsuccessful. Of course all this is true because the evolutionary process is always driven by diversity in both physical and behavioral (mental) aspects of life. To fight change in ourselves, or others, or in the times we live, is to ensure personal discontentment sets in. **IT IS OK TO MARCH TO THE BEAT OF A DIFFERENT DRUM SO LONG AS THIS BEAT IS IN TUNE WITH THE GOLDEN RULE.** A good amount of discontentment is built around resisting change—denying reality. Marriages often last when they shouldn't, friendships are often pretended past any realistic time; social advances are resisted, like the broadening of basic rights to groups previously denied such rights, etc. Those who go through life clinging to notions, dogmas, and cultural traditions of their youth simply make life miserable for themselves. Those who enter their terminational years and try to stay on the playing field, where those in their productive years are busy playing the game, will find themselves disgruntled, discouraged, and disdainful of the younger generation. There is absolutely nothing wrong with settling down on the sidelines and simply enjoying the 'new' players as a sort of entertainment—theatre, if you wish. Even in the worst scenarios, evolutionary time will sort it all out, and progress will continue, albeit lengthy setbacks can occur. "Time flies", we say. No, "Time stays, We go".

WHAT IS THERE REALLY TO BE ANGUISHED ABOUT? If God's created process of evolution has done amazingly well for millions of years, on what logical basis should we assume it will proceed any differently? This evolutionary process is an ever changing phenomenon replete with amazing advances, catastrophic events, periods of extinctions, extended periods of dormancy prior to new advances, etc. Neither is it logical to pretend we, as individuals, are personal favorites of God, entitled to any basis for special favoritism. I can pretend God likes me, or my family, or my country, or my race, or my mode of worship better than He does those different in any of these categories, but all of human history teaches otherwise. Our own personal experiences tell us otherwise. Those trapped in this mentality have only one recourse—to have faith that after death everything will be just peachy in some sort of heaven for them and all those of their ilk. I have never understood why, if God really likes someone personally so much, He would allow some really awful things to happen to them on this earth. We have all known some really good people to suffer horribly with the cruelest of fates.

I mentioned before that Abraham Lincoln is an example of a very contented person. It was only his solid attachment to the realities of life, and his firm adherence to the Golden Rule and Golden Rule politics in his life that enabled him to remain admirably functional during all the stress. Was his a happy life? NO.

Little in his personal life generated endless happiness. But he was imminently confident in his own mind of his reasoning powers and in his faith that right (The Golden Rule) makes might, which enabled him to be one of the most contented persons in history. If indeed, human reasoning power and adherence to the Golden Rule are the bricks upon which contentment is built, then Lincoln stands out here as one of the most contented people ever. Few people, if any, got very close to Lincoln. Remember contentment comes from within, others cannot give it to you.

Also, contentment comes with a normal range of human emotions. A contented person, such as Lincoln, could hardly have been expected to respond to the tragedies around him with any cavalier attitude. A contented person emits the right emotions at the right time for the right length of time. A lot of people understand right and wrong but find excuses not to act in ways, or support ways, which will actuate the right over the wrong. Lincoln tied his reasoning powers, which were exceptional, to his sense of justice for all. It is no wonder that more books have been written about Lincoln than any other person except Jesus. His personage represents a modern day pinnacle of reason and ethics. How could anyone top Lincoln in both categories?

Does serving as a soldier in an army generate contentment? After all, your mind is in high gear and you think you are putting your life on the line for a good cause. We need be careful here. Many people mentally are in high gear and think, or deceive themselves into thinking, that they are doing the right things. This, in itself, means little. **IT IS THE QUALITY OF YOUR REASONING** and the ethics **ACTED OUT** according to the Golden Rule which count. What tyrant in history has ever been a contented person? What rich person, seeped in wealth and not giving their excess wealth away has ever been a contented person?

Regarding soldiers, it should be remembered that most soldiers are in their formative years or early productive years. Their lives are more about excitement, achievement, recognition, the acquisition of money. Whether contentment can be achieved having survived a war depends on the nature of the war. A war in which a soldier is defending a country being invaded is an extremely selfless act. The citizens of the invaded country deeply appreciate the sacrifice others make to help them defend their sovereignty. For example, the strong kind feelings felt by the Europeans toward Americans after World War II lasted half a century.

In other wars since then, which are the vast majority of wars, the United States was the invading nation. In wars of this sort the invading soldiers are mostly resented. Sovereignty doesn't mean a lot if another country can invade to change your politics or religion or exploit your natural resources. Soldiers in scenarios like this aren't viewed by the locals as saving anyone but simply prevailing and creating massive physical and human devastation. Soldiers often enter the war seeing themselves as saviors, and, finding more resentment than gratitude, often develop an intense dislike of the 'natives'. Unlike during the World Wars, most United States citizens make no sacrifice, and are not susceptible to being drafted, and these modern wars are financed through borrowed money. Most Americans want to win these wars as a source of patriotic pride, but the gratitude toward the soldiers is relatively shallow, maybe a few quick reflections at halftime of a football game, etc. In many cases the average citizen is bewildered why anyone would sign up to be a mercenary in a war where there are no uniformed armies on a battlefield, and the biggest danger comes if, when you step in the wrong spot, some homemade bomb blows up in your vicinity, or some nondescript sniper kills you from a building window. Soldiers return home often mentally and emotionally impaired from the intense stress and from seeing so much senseless violence. Upon return they tend to become bitter, either because they feel they risked their lives for nothing, or feel they really were risking their lives for something and no one seems much to care. Rah, rah, bang, bang—thank you soldier—goodbye, now you are discharged. The loquacious praise from politicians seeking office rings hollow and the indifference from the general public leaves them frustrated and betrayed. So, no, our latest wars don't generate any contentment for most of the mercenaries who fought in these wars. It is nothing like the World Wars and the American Civil War in which all were fought on principle, all of age were draftable (you could, though, buy your way out in the Civil War), and everyone sacrificed for their cause.

If the Golden Rule is really the inherent basis for human ethics, then it is possible to roughly place people in group categories. Some people see life totally as a responsibility to their own welfare. A spouse is there to meet their needs, children are there to do as they tell them to do, etc. Others broaden their ethical mantra to include immediate family; others broaden it to include immediate family plus members of their particular religious faith and/or ethnic group/nation of residence etc. All of these people are hardly ethical in their behavior. In the purest sense the Golden Rule implies it is always the least fortunate amongst us who require the greatest amount of our shared excessive wealth. Excessive wealth has already been defined as wealth past the basic needs of living. Obviously there is a gray area of debate as to what constitutes BASIC, but quibbling over this is a distraction. If, for example, the basic cost of a car is $20,000 or $24,000 is not worth debating here. And we have already established if one wants to spend more on a car they can do so if what they spend to buy a more expensive car is met with an equal donation to those least fortunate. There is, however, no necessity for such unequal distribution of wealth as it exists today and certainly no reason why a Christian nation such as the United States should currently be leading the way among industrialized countries in a growing disparity between the rich and the middle class/poor. Sharing is the crux of human ethics. **PRAYING FOR THE POOR, THOSE DYING FROM CURABLE DISEASES, THE OPPRESSED, THE DIFFERENT, ETC IS AN EGREGIOUS COP-OUT**. This sort of exercise is nothing more than our demanding of God to do what God has given humans the ability to do themselves—collectively and individually. The trouble is that most of us simply do not want to part with our own excess wealth. And even if we are cautious and are saving it for a rainy day, then surely, when we die, it can go back into the society from which it came in order to help the least fortunate. Society here means the global community of life forms and natural resources. We ourselves are not special, our immediate family is not special, humans as a species are not special, and everything around us is governed by the same laws of evolution, a process created by God. The evolution of ethics over human history time has been progressive, albeit not in any straight line, nor at the same rate in different human societies. If, as postulated in this tractate, humans are behaving in a self destructive way, and if we cannot, at this time, correct our behavior in time, then there will be an evolutionary correction of some sort; the process of evolution and all the laws which govern this process will then proceed as this process has for billions of years. On what basis are we to assume the human species is the end product of this evolutionary process? We can understand much of the past, but comprehending what the future holds for God's created evolutionary process is beyond our reach. For a new advanced species to exist must the human species become extinct like the dinosaurs? Will we coexist with a more advanced species? Will other planets play a role in future life environments? It is a waste of time to predict the answer to any of these questions. We are not only not in charge, but we have not the intelligence to comprehend matters at such a level.

The best we can do is figure out what is the meaning of our individual lives. This musing suggests each of us strives to maximize contentment in our lives. To the extent we achieve this, the more successful our lives have been. How to achieve contentment has been postulated to be via the Golden Rule. The reward for ethical behavior is personal contentment and the betterment of life for the less fortunate. In this way contentment of varying degrees is reached for the maximum number of people. This is ethics. We all, everywhere, really do know this. We just need to focus on it and then act on it.

Chapter 21

A good deal of this musing has been written on a wing and a prayer. That is to say, one forges ahead with a topic that has no clear edges, no clear comprehension of just how universally applicable all this is, and an admitted understanding that all of this is based on organized assemblage by just one person. My assumption here is that others would have to tweak all this a bit to make it a smooth fit with their own lives. If diversity is the reality of life, then one could argue contentment comes via diverse pathways. Still, observation seems to refute this. While contentment is one of degrees, the pathway to contentment does not seem all that varied. Where are these people so contented who do not follow the Golden Rule in their lives? They may be wealthy, they may have a lot of power, they may have religious titles, they may be popular, they may be energetic, they may have the best of looks, the brightest of brains, BUT there is never any evidence of personal contentment in the absence of using reason and the Golden Rule as the basis for personal behavior. These are, instead, angry people, combative individuals, self serving leaches on society, always grabbing more than ever giving, and the lot of the least fortunate is hardly, or ever, improved by their actions in life—absent pure coincidence.

What now follows, as a form of summary, are the basic insights discussed here, formulated as some form of practical game plan:

Achieving Contentment, as the meaning of life, is somewhat age dependent. During our formative years it is emotions which govern our lives as we learn basic ways to function in life. Life is complicated for humans, and thus the formative years are long. In the formative years we have emotional extremes—we squeal with joy, we cry with frustration, we get real angry, real sad, etc. How many times, in later years, do we look back and miss the ability to get so purely excited about something? Or be in 'love' so intensely, or be so thoughtlessly impulsive? We all had rather raw edges back then, maybe not in the same way, to the same extent, but in a relative way, compared to our later years.

In our productive years achievements and amassing wealth play a major role, again to varying degrees. Personal interactions and family matters are way up there too. Power, titles, income, and **THINGS** of all sorts tend to gain center stage. There are many exceptions. Some, at a young age, solve the personal contentment puzzle, and live contented lives during their productive years. Probably most, however, seem to wallow in the shallow end of the contentment pool, submerged to varying degrees in the 'rat race'.

When the productive years are over and the Terminational stage of life begins, there is but one goal worth pursuing—**CONTENTMENT**. This will either be the stage of life where contentment settles in, or the remaining years will be sad, painful, frustrating—bathed in misery and regret, fearing death, and angry at our current fate in life. If we have lived a long life, the pieces of life's puzzle are scattered throughout our lives. If we cannot put these pieces together to get a decent understanding of God's evolutionary process we will continue to think of ourselves as the center of importance. We all want to be important, and in a minuscule way we are, but we are never the center of importance—nor the focus of God's personal attention, no matter how much we may wish to be. We are all as but one brick in the most beautiful and magnificent building ever. The brick is part of the magnificence and beauty, but not as an individual brick. Bricks can't reason or feel, but we can, and it is only natural that we resent this fact, and want ourselves to be special, to be the center of attention. This requires an attitude adjustment. It was chance that gave all of us the opportunity to be a part of life, to strut on life's stage for a minuscule period of time. It is never a forced sort of participation. We can end our lives at any time, certain religious notions notwithstanding. The notion that God decides when or how any individual dies is simply preposterous unless you mean God created the laws which govern evolution.

IF WE DON'T EVER COME TO UNDERSTAND OUR ROLE IN EVOLUTION, WE CAN NEVER GAIN PERSONAL CONTENTMENT. We can get self-servingly silly and start claiming God gave us dominion over all other species, that God—for whatever imagined reason—is personally protecting us and guiding us through life; He even has reserved a place for us in some sort of heaven. Illusions seldom last. At some point people who go this route end up asking, "God, why hast thou forsaken me?". Understanding plus accepting reality is part of maturing, and personal contentment is never going to come without this personal maturation. We were dealt certain cards genetically and environmentally. If we are not the most beautiful human specimen, or the smartest, or the most athletic, or have the best personality, or were born in the best of all environments, in the best of all times—well, we have to use whatever cards we have to do the very best we can, and hope that enough people will live enough by the Golden Rule to make life a more level playing field—so we too, can have a chance for some success, given our personal and environmental limitations. God's evolutionary process has given the human species the ability to help themselves and others. **SURVIVAL OF THE FITTEST HAS BEEN GREATLY MODIFIED BY OUR HUMAN ABILITY TO REASON AND OUR INHERENT SENSE OF ETHICS**. Many people, with limited personal talents, live contented lives because others have shared their better blessings to enable these less fortunate to live better lives.

I am 70+ years of age. This to me, as I am sure to many others of similar years, is absolutely astounding. Anyone who gets 50 years of a good life has no reason to complain. Every good year after that is a bonus. Thus, reaching 70, I already have 20 years of bonus. With rapid medical advancements it may well be common for people to live to be 100. If that sounds great, a little more thought probably needs to be given on this. **QUALITY OF LIFE IS NO SMALL MATTER.** If we are going to live to be 100 someone has to financially support us. All these amazing medical advancements which can keep us alive longer and longer are very expensive. We can patch, patch, patch ever more successfully, BUT none of this is making us younger, just keeping us alive longer. The financial cost, the cost on natural resources, the stress placed on our family caregivers—all of this is a heavy cost. People often state, "If I can be healthy I would love to live to be 100." Really, what person in their nineties do we know who is healthy? They are nothing but a shell of their former selves. I guess by healthy we mean they are not in pain, can still get around of sorts, and can still have rational thoughts some of the time. This is simply disingenuous. Almost all the things they were once so good at are gone. Gone with the wind. My dad lived to be 89 and my mother 97, and for their ages, would have been called healthy. The most notable change in the lives of the elderly is increasing helplessness. And just when they are becoming helpless their mate dies and one of them is supposed to carry on alone at a point in their lives when they are least capable of functioning on their own. **HUMAN LIFE IS NOT VALUED BECAUSE THERE ARE SOME LIVING CELLS**. All living things have some living cells. A horrible human fate is to be alive but mostly 'dead' from the neck up, or to be in such poor health that quality of life becomes a negative score. That point is not fixed in granite, and each person will arrive to that point at different times. What is hell on earth for one may not be for another.

Our lives cannot be contented until we understand our own importance in God's created evolutionary process. This understanding is called coming to grips with reality. **LIFE IS NOT BASED ON WHAT WE WANT, OR WHAT OUR CHILDREN WANT, OR WHAT OUR COUNTRY WANTS**; life is not based on our being 'special' in the sense of having God negate His own created laws of evolution in order to protect us from varied potential misfortunes; life is not a matter of 'good' versus 'evil'; life is about individual uniqueness; life is foremost about a progressive advancement in the complexity of life; life is about change and the only permanence is Time; life is about chance, diversity and change, the two parameters of our existence which will impact our lives from the get-go.

We got a chance at life by chance, and all we have ever been given is an opportunity, by chance, to participate in the evolutionary process. That's it, nothing more, nothing less. Our role in the process is so minuscule that it would be preposterous to claim we are special. We do have the opportunity to fare better or worse with the cards we were dealt, but not, as we are oft to claim, "by doing it solely the old fashioned way, earning it". The goal in life is singular for all of us—to achieve a state of contentment. For most species the singular goal is survival—survival of the fittest. The fittest survive, the gene pool becomes enriched, progress ever so slowly is achieved.

The human species is unique in that we have an inherent sense of ethics—an ethics based on reasoning, not programmed neuronal circuitry. This inherited inherent sense of ethics is still in the early stages of evolving, and **THERIN LIES OUR LIMITATIONS**. Any of us who have studied the process of evolution can understand the sequence of progress—**BUT**, trying to imagine the nature of new species in the future is mind-boggling. Are we the last new species? Will the human species become extinct and be replaced? What new traits are left to be developed? Will the evolutionary process never end or is there a final end point, past which no more evolution can occur? We can ask these questions but we will find no answers.

With any individual human life, for a full cycle to occur, we have to pass through our formative years, our productive years, and our terminational years. The beginning and end of these stages may vary from person to person, but the stages are always there short of death prior to a stage. The formative years are crucial, depend heavily on the cards we are dealt, and these cards set the odds for the rest of our lives. We need always be mindful that we did not choose our parents, did not choose our formative environment, did not choose our physical appearance, did not choose the grade and high schools we attended, did not choose our potential neighborhood peers, did not choose our religion, did not choose our intellectual potential, did not choose our basic personality, did not choose our athletic potential, etc. This is one of the first reality checks: life is not a level playing field. It is not a level playing field because **EVOLUTION CAN'T**

PROGRESS WITH A LEVEL PLAYING FIELD, and IT IS THE EVOLUTIONARY PROCESS WHICH IS IMPORTANT, NOT ANY OF US AS INDIVIDUALS.

We all tend to view success as accumulating money and/or material things; as achieving popularity; as achieving control, power, titles, reputation, sex, a good marriage etc. None of these parameters are evil, just not the road to contentment. They may enrich life, create temporary spurts of happiness, but they are not, in themselves, any road to contentment. The mistake occurs when any of these become viewed as the means to contentment or contentment itself. Contentment is always the goal of our lives by definition of the word.

Our formative years represent genetic potential and a lot of environmental luck. These are the years of challenge, of emotional highs and lows, frustrations, powerlessness, acquired or inherited personal prejudices, social ineptitude, and maximum adaptive flexibility. This stage in life is our training stage, and by definition it is the others who do the training—parents, peers, teachers, clergy, coaches, etc. Thus, we are in essence "us" by a genetic toss of the dice, and we become a matured "us" via other means. To the extent the number and quality of others in our lives is limited, our potential to be a productive member of society is stunted. We learn a lot quickly and often **TENTATIVELY** in our formative years.

Early childhood is extremely important. In theory, no really caring society ever leaves a child in a poor environment. In reality, we often get downright silly—like insisting every fertilized egg must be brought to term under some sanctity of life banner. Sanctity of life is not exactly a focus of the evolutionary process. Variety and quality of life are foci of the evolutionary process—death of individual species members is a natural part of this process. To bring to term a child with no proper environment to nurture that child in his/her formative years is as antisocial an act as murder. Today, with human overpopulation of the globe, to bring to term more than two fertilized eggs per female, is likewise as antisocial an act as murder. Overpopulation creates cruel miseries to huge populations of human beings, especially young defenseless children. Adults can fight for a piece of the pie, children get what they get. **THE HUMAN SPECIES, IN THEORY, HAS THE INTELLIGENCE TO FREE ITSELF FROM SURVIVAL OF THE FITTEST TO A SUBSTANTIAL DEGREE.** Humans have enough reasoning power to help level the playing field, thus reducing the cruelty of any survival of the fittest process, and to control its own population growth.

Because of our inherent ethical nature, almost all of us understand right and wrong. Only those with certain mental deficiencies are devoid of this comprehension. **NO ONE, ANYWHERE, DISPUTES THE VALIDITY OF THE GOLDEN RULE AS AN ETHICAL PRINCIPLE.** Ethical behavior is a universally inherited concept, not dependent on some parental inherited religion. We understand why we have invented religion—to give us a personal advantage in life; to find protection from dangers in life; to find a way to alleviate any responsibility for unethical behavior. Genuine ethical behavior, the kind dictated by the Golden Rule, is not only difficult to practice, it presents obstacles in many of the pathways of life we choose to follow. There is nothing wrong with desiring to be affluent, to seek power, to seek popularity, to feel a strong attachment to your own offspring, to have sexual desires, to gamble, to use recreational drugs, to want to win at sports or any other contest, to love to eat, to have hobbies, etc. BUT, and this is the key—we always need to develop a realization as to when **ENOUGH IS ENOUGH**. If we fail to do this, then contentment cannot be attained, no matter what the object of our pursuit is. In some very real sense, when we do not understand when enough is enough, then those others with the greatest needs will never get enough. Any ethical entity involves the recognition of right and wrong. Right and wrong dictate the existence of reward and punishment. If there is no reward or punishment then there is no purpose of behaving ethically. Contentment in our life is the reward.

We don't always want to do right. Ethics can be a real nuisance to us on many occasions—an immediate stumbling block to the pursuit of many things we value. We thus latch on to something which might enable us to both pursue something and be ethical- **–OR AT LEAST** have some sort of way where we can be forgiven for our sins. Religion often teaches us that the reward for ethical behavior comes after death, some sort of heaven. Of course invented religions would do this—after all, if the reward follows here right now in our life, then where the hell is it? If a person goes to church faithfully, practices all the proper rituals, is pleasant enough to others, then why are there so many disappointments, tragedies, and sufferings in their lives? Well, according to human invented religion, the reward will come in some sort of after-death heaven. And just to ensure we don't simply take a pass, there has to be punishment after death for sinners- –some sort of hell. Based on reason alone, all this is rather silly. Reason is based on evidence, and of course we have no evidence whatsoever about any life after death. Thus invented religion has to place FAITH as a cornerstone of achieving this heaven after death. Such faith is stressed a lot in our lives. The most horrible things can happen to the best of people and it becomes really hard to understand how this could possibly be fair. "God operates in mysterious ways" is another way of admitting total lack of understanding as to why bad things happen to good people, however we may define good here. Faith cannot stand by itself as a form of comfort. Invented religion now has to incorporate forgiveness. It is not helpful to have an all or none situation with ethical behavior. Who wants to feel, "Uh oh, I screwed up and sinned, I am now going to hell and there is nothing I can do about it." This would leave everyone depressed rather early in life. So forgiveness has to be invented—thus we have confessions, being 'saved', trade-offs, and sometimes all sorts of points are gained by destroying or 'saving' the heathens—those whose inherited or by marriage religion differs from our own inherited or by marriage religion. This inherited religion stuff comes with some serious baggage, both to ourselves and to others, especially the heathens. Almost all suicide 'bombers' are very religious. It is not so much a heroic act as an act of final desperation. Nothing is right in their lives; all options seem exhausted, and any real reason why heaven will be their destination seems elusive **UNLESS** they sacrifice their own lives to 'take out' some of the heathens who need to be punished for their actions against the 'true religion'.

At some point we enter our productive years, albeit how productive varies widely from person to person. There may be genetic limitations, social limitations or environmental limitations. Maturation always depends on input coupled with potential. A person born with an opaque cornea cannot see as an adult even if the cornea is surgically replaced. To mature properly, input has to come during the formative stage in life. Since diversity is the cornerstone of the evolutionary process, the productive years, taking in the total population of humans in that stage at any one time, become a real hodgepodge of genetic diversity operating in varied environmental enclaves. Humans have a genetically determined ethical component, in part, because our intelligence magnifies the perception of pain. We, more so than any other species, understand the possible consequences of pain and also the concept of death. These two comprehensions make survival of the fittest exceptionally cruel for humans. To reduce the cruelty level inherent in survival of the fittest, humans also have genetically inherent ethics—the Golden Rule. Wherever the Golden Rule rules, the cruelty generated by the survival of the fittest is lessened. Because of the Golden Rule, if we are not the fittest, we don't have to suffer so much because others can make life more pleasant for us. And the others who do so, the ones who have life advantages but understand when enough is enough for them, and understand their duty to the less fortunate, will help make the playing field of life more fair for more people. The reward these giving people gain will be contentment, and contentment is the goal and meaning of life. We all probably understand we can't take any of our money, our possessions, our titles, our power, our abilities, our bodies, or any of the other things about our lives that we value with us when we die. Thus, by definition, all these things which we pursue in our productive years are temporary, never end-points in life. The end point in all our lives is personal contentment, and only the Golden Rule, conscientiously followed as our #1 priority, can bring us a level of contentment. Any human being, no matter their status in life, can practice the Golden Rule. Some of the most ethical people I have known in life had very little going for them in terms of advantages, but were relatively content in life and were a pleasure to be around. I have never been the most social person on the planet, but I enjoy most being around those people with whom there is no need to watch my back, compete for something, or be anything other than myself and let them be themselves.

This brings up another aspect of our productive and terminational years. Diversity, the cornerstone of the evolutionary process, breeds human personalities which don't really mesh that well with each other in many cases. So what? This is to be expected. Diversity, by its purpose for existing, is a good thing. Live and let live is part of the Golden Rule. You don't like the way somebody else dresses or wears their hair, or their unique personality, or the way they live their life, or with whom they are married or with whom they associate.? That's ok. You don't have to like how they live their lives. You only have to give them the same rights and considerations you expect in life.

The evolution of ethics in the human species seems to proceed more rapidly than physical evolution. Of course physical evolution is going on too. Modern day athletes in any sport are stronger, faster, bigger, and better than athletes from ages past. Yet ethics has progressed also. We don't burn people at the stake anymore or quarter them, which is not to say some of the Cheney-ites in our world are not still fixated ethically at that level. But women have gotten rights, slavery is mostly abolished, blacks and other minorities have gained rights, gays are now gaining rights, children have some protections, and the list goes on. As time passes the list of personal prejudices prevalent around the globe get fewer and fewer. **ORGANIZED RELIGION, BY ITS VERY NATURE, IS THE LAST TO ACCEPT DIVERSITY.** If God is personally on our side and we have faith in all the rituals and prejudices of our inherited or by marriage religion, it is rather difficult to change without considering it a breach of holy faith. That is the conundrum those with faith in their religion face: if something in the scripture of their religion, always written by some human in the past, is wrong, how do they know what else might be wrong? Religious purists are trapped: it's the all or none law-—it is either all right or none of it can be trusted to be right. The Pope is either God's appointed emissary to humans on our planet or he isn't. If he is, then everything he says is right or wrong must be right or wrong. If God had nothing to do with who ends up being the Pope then nothing the Pope says has any more validity than what others may be saying. God's evolutionary process has given humans the ability to reason, to accumulate knowledge from one generation to the next, and therein lies the basis for our progress, including the evolution of ethics, all this occurring as we live today.

Diversity is a major player in evolution and this diversity leads to change. **CHANGE IS A CONSTANT IN THE EVOLUTIONARY PROCESS**. If we don't learn to accept this and understand the value and purpose of change, it is difficult to reach contentment. Almost everything we value in life will be gone or changed with time. Parents, friends, spouses, workmates, mentors, etc., are never relationships fixed in stone. These relationships change with time and in a zillion different ways for a zillion different reasons. There is little point in reacting to these changes with anger and accusations. A friend does not owe you lasting friendship, neither does a spouse, etc. The value of all friendships, of all ilk, is the richness they give to our lives at some point—the support, the respect, the positive contribution to our own understanding of life. When relationships change they change, period. They can become stable, they can become stronger, they can become weaker, they can become insufferable. None of us can force anyone to like us. If we reserve the right to find someone else not our cup of tea, we need grant others the right to find us not their cup of tea. Fair is fair. Most relationships are fleeting, change with time, and are more like two ships passing in the night, a brief interaction, and then both ships sail on. Marriage failures are especially difficult because the investment was so great with children involved. Each marital breakup is different, and the best each spouse can do is be realistic and fair. When anger enters, both realism and fairness disappear. I suppose there is nothing better than a good marriage and nothing worse than a bitter divorce. The nature of all marriages most likely changes with time. The reasons for staying together vary all over the place. Observing varied marriages and how these diverse marriages function is a genuine soap opera. No one claims life is easy. Conflicts abound from every direction. **HOWEVER**, our own sense of values and priorities can lend a kind of consistency which, through our ethical values, can keep us both sane and contented to varying degrees in our lives.

The Golden Rule is simple enough in theory to understand, but very difficult to adhere to in practice. Nowhere is this more true than in our relationships with family, especially offspring. The obligation to help the less fortunate is part of the Golden Rule. If this is not part of the Golden Rule then nothing is. Every major religion preaches it is a virtue to help the less fortunate. **BUT, FOR THE MOST PART, IN PRACTICE, IT IS MOSTLY SMOKE AND MIRRORS**. Right now today, the distribution of wealth in our own country is becoming more concentrated in the hands of the wealthy than in any other industrialized country. Globally, in terms of raw numbers, there are more people on earth today dying from hunger, from treatable diseases, from poor water sources, from homelessness, from lack of work to make a living, than in any other period in history. The Golden Rule implies if you have excess wealth above the basics to live a healthy and prosperous life, that excess must go to help the less fortunate. To the extent it is true that we are not 'special' beings ourselves, that we are just as much controlled by the laws of evolution as any other individual life form, then it would be irrational to view any others as exempt from not being 'special'—and this includes our children. This understandable and strong bond between parents and their children often becomes the major obstacle for us to follow the Golden Rule.

Let's say we become fairly successful in life and have excess wealth beyond our basic needs. Who gets this excess wealth and when? It would be hard to become successful and affluent if one, from the get-go, gives away excess wealth as it first appears. We all know money begets money—the more you have, the easier it is to accumulate even more. There is no real reason to cease striving to advance our economic wealth in life. This is not evil or wrong. The question that does reign, however, is just what are we to do with our accumulated wealth? No religious prophet of which I am aware, including Jesus, ever approved the hoarding of wealth—not by an individual, not by a family tree, not by a corporation, and not by any economic, social, or ethnic group. **THE HOARDING OF WEALTH IS UNETHICAL, WHETHER WE FOLLOW SCRIPTURE OF ORGANIZED RELIGION OR THE GODLEN RULE.** Earning wealth is one thing, hoarding it is quite another thing. To use the advantages we are given in life to become affluent is fair enough. By the Creator's design, nothing is ever equal in the evolutionary process. But, we humans have a strong ethical component in our genetic makeup. **TO HOARD WEALTH, IN ANY SOCIETY, IS TO LEAVE THAT WEALTH INACCESSIBLE TO THE LESS FORTUNATE, WHO NEED A REASONABLE DISTRIBUTION OF WEALTH IN THEIR SITUATION FOR THEM TO PROSPER—IN MANY CASES FOR THEM TO EVEN SURVIVE.** We now live in a world that is overpopulated with humans, with natural resources inadequate for such a staggering population. This, coupled with the hoarding of wealth by the few at the expense of the many, has produced crises for humanity unparalleled during the existence of humans on the planet.

It is our collective failure to honor the Golden Rule which has enabled such a situation to develop. Personal rights are always secondary to the welfare of society as a whole. Period. We may wish to drive a 100 miles an hour but this endangers the lives of others. So we can't. If we don't want others to drive at 100 miles an hour then we ourselves cannot do so. That is the Golden Rule. If human overpopulation is a tragedy for human society, then responsible reproduction is mandated for everyone. To excuse any person from responsible reproduction is ethically absurd; to say birth control is a sin is an illogical outrageous fabrication. To bring a child to term, when the situation is such that no proper care for the child is likely,—is a sin, and hardly a minor sin either. The sanctity of life concept has no basis in reality. Those who preach this babble apparently envision a God who decides who shall exist and when they shall die, etc. Well, for these people to be correct about the sanctity of life then God Himself would never let anyone die, and certainly not His 'favorites'. Life certainly has a purpose and meaning, but it is transient for everyone, no exceptions. When in history has God decided any human, due to the sanctity of life, should not die? Never. So much for God's belief in the sanctity of life, at least as we tend to define life. Well, the religious purists might say, life goes on after death. Really? Well then, using the same logic, the life of a fetus, not brought to term, will go on to Heaven; this fetus will bypass all the stress of earthly existence and go directly to Heaven. I think that would be just fine with about all concerned. At any rate, **THE WELFARE OF ALL DICTATES THAT EVERYONE BE REQUIRED TO PRACTICE RESPONSIBLE REPRODUCTION.** Hey, we license all kinds of human behaviors, put limits on them, and to do the same with reproduction is hardly a sin, but an essential action to avert all the disasters that accompany over-population of any species. **WE HUMANS HAVE THIS TENDENCY TO THINK WE RUN THE SHOW, HAVE DOMINION OVER OTHER SPECIES, ARE A FAVORED SPECIES BY GOD HIMSELF, WITH THE FAVORED AND SAVED AMONGST US GOING ON TO HEAVEN.** All the evidence we have gained through our power to reason has made rather clear that the human species is governed by the same laws of evolution which govern all other species.

It is well to remember this: **THE PURPOSE OF ETHICS AS A GENETIC TRAIT OF HUMANS IS TO ENABLE THE MOST MEMBERS OF THE SPECIES AS POSSIBLE TO RECEIVE GOOD MEDICAL CARE, ADEQUATE FOOD, SHELTER, OPPORTUNITY FOR WORK, THE SAME RIGHTS IN LIFE AS OTHERS, INDIVIDUAL FREEDOMS, SECURITY FROM HARM, A GOOD EDUCATION, SOCIAL SUPPORT, ETC.** It is not possible to be religious, if religion includes ethics, without this being the goal of ethical living. Taking care of ourselves and our family, friends, country, etc., is of course an admirable and necessary duty. It doesn't do that much good to 'take care of' others who will not strive to take care of themselves. It is a two sided equation. **HOWEVER**, it is no simple equation, it is no level field equation. Those of us with the most advantages end up with a greater responsibility to share our 'wealth' with the less advantaged. And the 'others' is never limited to our own families, our own friends, our own country, our own religion, our own culture, our own socioeconomic class, or any other grouping. There is no evidence in evolutionary history, or even human history, that God has favorites. We can, I reckon, make the assumption that whoever is gaining or coming out on top is God's favorite and He is interceding to ensure His favorite side is gaining or coming out on top. **YET**, this is illogical. According to this notion, during the first half of World War II God was on Hitler's side and then He switched sides. This would be kind of strange. And God must then surely have hated the American Indians. In fact God didn't take any chances from the get-go. He arranged to have most of them wiped out by diseases they were not immune to so that there would be no real military contest, especially since God arranged for the invaders to have guns. The Indians He gave bow and arrows. If this had an inkling of truth to it, what kind of God are we creating in our minds? Religion gets reduced then to a sorry-ass soap opera. Any attempt by any of us to believe we are special individuals or groups in God's plans is so clearly self-serving as to be childish in nature. There is no sanctity of life in terms of individual members of any species. We are all dead in the long run. God created a most impressive process, a timeless process, and a process that has yielded astounding results and progress. We can imagine the process is about us individually, or our family, or our culture, or our inherited religion, or our country, or anything else we might throw in here—**BUT**, there is simply no rational basis to conclude any such thing. All the evidence points in the other direction.

Furthermore, we cannot make ourselves more important, or our children more important, or our culture more important, or our nation more important, or our inherited religion more important to God's scheme of evolution by **SIMPLY STATING SUCH A THING AS A MATTER OF FAITH**. We can create all sorts of rituals, make up scriptures of various ilk, pass laws which give us official higher standing in our society, kill others titled heathens, etc., but none of this is based on any rational evidence that any of us are indeed special favored players in the process of evolution. All we can do is utilize our inherent ethical capabilities to live the Golden Rule. To the extent we do this we can achieve various degrees of contentment in life. And this is the goal everyone seeks to achieve. Now what could possibly be more important to us in life than to achieve a degree of contentment? **CONTENTMENT IS NOT THE ROAD TO ANYWHERE, IT IS THE TERMINATION POINT**. Everything else we do, we do precisely to achieve as much contentment as possible. The object is not to be enticed to going down the wrong roads—the dead-enders.

All of this leads us to the most difficult understanding of all. Almost all of us understand the need to share our blessings with others. The problem is, for all practical purposes that often becomes essentially limited to our spouses, our kids, our own religion, our own country, our own ethnic group, etc. The word **OTHER** does not mean any others of our choosing. It refers to those least fortunate in life. If we are not ourselves 'special' beings in the eyes of God (special meaning compared to others) then of course neither are our spouse, our children, our country, our ethnic group, etc. special in that respect either. **CONSEQUENTLY**, if we amass a million dollars and pass this million dollars off to anyone who is not in the category of 'less fortunate', we are not ethical. Doing this is akin to saying we will not share with others because we want the surplus for ourselves or our own cabal of some sort. We all know, we really do, that this is unethical and if this selfishness is not wrong, then nothing much is wrong. **THERE IS NO WAY WE CAN REPLACE THE LEAST FORTUNATE WITH SELECT OTHERS IN OUR LIVES AND GIVE OUR SURPLUS WEALTH TO THESE SELECT OTHERS**. In makes no difference who the 'select others' are; doing this is unethical.

We have trapped ourselves in this country into a terrible bind. Out of deep affection to those closest to us, either emotionally or genetically, we have made it the norm to give almost all our excess wealth to others outside the least fortunate. Because it is now considered by most to be the norm, children would be incensed to find out mom and pop are giving their excess wealth to the less fortunate, not to them. Of course, if any of our offspring are in the category of 'least fortunate' that is different. **OUR SOCIETY IS AT FAULT FOR LETTING OFFSPRING EXPECT TO GET PARENTAL WEALTH UPON THE DEATH OF A PARENT**. If this were not an expected event, children would not get their noses out of joint when the 'least fortunate' got that excess wealth. And a hell of a lot more siblings would be on speaking terms with each other after the parents are dead—the battle for the family fortune would have no need to exist. What kind of American value have we instituted? I thought the goal was for each person to become a productive member of society earning his or her own little nest egg. Thus, it would seem, hoarding wealth in a family tree is both unethical and un-American. We can, and often do, twist ourselves into a pretzel denying any such obligation, and wrap ourselves is some sort of supposed ethical cocoon called 'family values'. God's created evolutionary process has given God a huge family of 'beings', from the simplest to the most complicated, from those long deceased, to those ever present right now. What logical reason exists for us to think that God does not expect humans to use their inherited sense of ethics to help the less fortunate of humanity and protect the natural resources available to sustain all forms of life? If we cannot eradicate misfortune from the evolutionary process, we can at least lessen the burden on the less fortunate. This, it is reasoned here, is not only God's intent, but gives to all those who follow this Golden Rule, what we all seek—personal contentment.

The solution here is self-evident. When children learn early on that their parents believe accumulated excess wealth is ethically required to go to the less fortunate, they not only are exposed to this ethical principle, but never begin to set their sights on a huge inheritance. Only when children are led to believe they are in line for any excess wealth of their parents, are they going to find their noses out of joint later down the line.

While Jesus and all the prophets in major religions have made this clear enough, often enough, organized religion has failed here pretty much across the board. This is no small failure. The consequences of allowing wealth to accumulate in genetic cabals has led directly to the wide disparity of wealth distribution in the human population. We all know that the more wealth we have, the easier it is to accumulate more wealth. That increased accumulation has to come from others. At some point, in about every major empire in history, more and more of the middle class become poor as the appetite of the already wealthy grows larger and larger. America faces that right now. Strangely, so far even when an initiative is on the ballot to raise the taxes of the wealthy or plug up the loopholes which allows the wealth to amass even more wealth, the voters reject it. The rejection follows political ads which carefully prey upon the ignorance of many voters via manipulating propaganda which is designed to activate the prejudices and fears of many voters. These voters then vote against the ballot initiative for reasons which have nothing to do with the purpose of the initiative. At any rate, until our culture changes, via organized religion, or via other groups, it ends up hard for people to be ethical with their excess accumulated wealth.

It is not unreasonable to expect offspring to earn their own way after their formative years, around 18 or so. To "earn our own way" is an essential part of our productive years and a basic American value. The more someone else 'hands' you your wealth the more apt you are to be discontented. **SOMEONE ELSE CAN HAND YOU A TITLE, MONEY, A JOB, POWER, JUST BECAUSE THEY ARE IN A POSITION TO DO SO**. It is like the old saying, "Give me a fish and I eat for a day; teach me to fish and I eat for a lifetime." Much of organized religion is about giving people a fish to eat. This, of course, is short-sighted and no solution. Of course things like soup kitchens are worth-while and noble, but true ethics demands much more involvement—with time or money. **ETHICS IS ABOUT ENABLING THE LESS FORTUNATE TO COMPETE MORE SUCCESSFULLY IN LIFE ON A MORE LEVEL PLAYING FIELD**. A reasonable distribution of wealth in a society is not welfare, not relieving anyone of personal responsibility, not a blessing to the less fortunate via trickle down, or any of the other excuses people use to avoid ethical responsibility to other humans. No, **A REASONABLE DISTRIBUTION OF WEALTH IS SOCIAL FAIRNESS**. We cannot tie some people with one hand behind their backs and call it a fair contest. If we can't be happy enough to be affluent, and need to hoard surplus wealth ourselves, or in a family tree, or any other 'tree', then we are not ethical. Really, the best parents are those who make every effort to enable their offspring to generate their own economic affluence as adults, not removing pressure for them to do so by ensuring they understand economic support for them is a life long commitment. No one really wins with this sort of self-assigned importance.

What percentage of time should we spend advancing our own efforts to be affluent versus what percentage of time should we spend supporting and working with those in need of more justice and a more level playing field? It is hard, when younger, to focus too much on the needs of others when we are so heavily engaged in trying to better ourselves. How well, or how soon, we ever come to understand the nature of life impacts on when, or if, we ever develop our full ethical potential and realize the relationship between ethics (the Golden Rule) and contentment in our lives. The world is not so much driven by evil versus good as it is by chance, diversity, and, in the case of the human species--the ethics of others. None of us is an island unto ourselves. We know this. For us to say any successes of ours, however minuscule or huge they might be, fall under some sort of "we earned them" is disingenuous. No, let's be a bit more honest. I inherited certain genes, inherited a certain environment and historical time of birth, and, mostly by chance, I encountered others whose contributions to my life impacted tremendously on any of my successes. That's the way it is, that's the way it works, that's the nature of this game called life (the evolutionary process), as it functions via God's created laws of evolution.

Let us not fall into a fatal intellectual trap. There is no reason at all for us to assume God thinks like us, or finds us individually any kind of favorite. Of course we would like that, I certainly would. It would make life a breeze. There is no way, at our intellectual level, that something can come from nothing. It is a contradiction in terms. Yet, just as obviously, that had to have happened. In the end, where did God come from? How can the creator of everything—Himself—have come from nothing? This conundrum reflects the limitation of human understanding. Because we have conceptual limitations is no reason to discard rational thought as the basis for what we perceive to be correct. Because we cannot understand everything hardly justifies 'faith based' beliefs on ethics or any other aspect of our lives which have no reasonable basis for them. What is faith-based religion but an admission that, since we can't understand everything about life, we will simply believe whatever we think is in our own personal best interest. And that often reduces itself to a belief that faith in our birth- inherited, or marriage-inherited, religion provides divine protection from the land mines in life.

We have said throughout this treatise that we need develop an understanding of our own situation in life, about the nature of life, and our relationship to God's process of evolution. Only then can we fully develop our inherent ethical potential. Our ethical potential isn't something we can change anymore than we can change any other of our inherent characteristics. Each of us really is unique because of our genetics, our environment, and our experiences. What we have postulated throughout all this is that only developing our ethical potential can lead to contentment in our lives. **CONTENTMENT IS THE END POINT, NOT A STEP TO ACHIEVE ANYTHING ELSE.**

Perhaps achieving contentment is more difficult now than in the past. For those of us living in an affluent society we are surrounded by a zillion THINGS. Things for this, things for that, things for status, things for pleasure, things to make work easier, things to communicate, things to amuse us, things to increase our knowledge, just things, things—everywhere, and not a minute to spare. And therein lies a problem. **A CERTAIN AMOUNT OF SOLITUDE AND PERSONAL TIME IS NEEDED TO SORT OUT THE MEANING OF LIFE AND FOR OUR ETHICAL NATURE TO EVOLVE.** How much time a particular person needs in solitude to do this varies, but one **NEEDS TO ARRIVE AT A PLACE IN TIME WHERE ONE NEVER FEELS LESS ALONE THAN WHEN ALONE.** The one aspect of life that is lifelong is your own mental essence. Everything else comes and goes, but your own mental self is with you till death do you part. Solitude is the environment necessary for mental growth about life—a time to tumble around in our minds all the experiences and knowledge we keep receiving into our minds. Too many today suffer from useless information overload and woeful lack of understanding about life itself. When I see someone in a grocery store discussing on a cell phone what brand of peas to buy, I tend to think, "There is someone with a simple undeveloped mind." Riding on a train, or in other situations, we cannot help but hear some inane shallow conversations. Trivial shit, that's what most of it is, and it makes me rededicate my efforts to keep the trivial aspects of my life to a minimum. After a day watching mindless television ('reality' shows, sitcoms, trashy court cases and 'talent' bashing twitter), tweeting, messaging, cell phoning, computer gaming, idle chit chatting, mindless tasks at work—what the hell kind of mental development have we achieved? How, in any measurable way has our understanding of life been enhanced? What have we done which has increased our insight about life, or enabled us to appreciate the diversity and wonder of the world in which we live? For myself, a day without communion with nature, observing diverse people and places, reading nonfiction, writing, postulating, sumptuous eating, music, and pets is a lost day. A younger person might add sex, but that category is beyond rational discussion.

Anthony Store has probably done the best job placing solitude in the right perspective concerning human life. So this is a good point to incorporate some of his observations into this treatise. Store suggests our lives can be divided into our social relationships (humans are social animals) and our introspective mental processes. Both are necessary to achieve a contented life. There has probably been an over emphasis on the social aspects of life as the road to contentment. And modern life, with a multitude of material things piled ever higher and higher, makes it less likely we will find the time to be in touch with our innermost feelings, abilities, limitations, and our relationship to the evolutionary process. Most people probably have such a limited understanding of the evolutionary process, which has been underway now for millions of years, as to make it even possible for them to deny it exists. The ignorance here is abysmal. It really is, and has been replaced by inherited faith based human contrived rituals and human written scriptures. Creating a God to meet our immediate emotional needs has always been popular in every age and every culture.

The behaviors we exhibit can be reflex (simple or complex), faith based, dictated by others, or reasoned behavior. Time is needed to mull all the input to our minds and this time is an essential component of reasoned behavior. For many of us, buried in today's information overload, there is less time for mulling anything over. A lot of it becomes garbage in, garbage out.

Much of life revolves around changes which continually take place in our environment and within our own comprehension of reality. None of us is the same person over time. Some, of course, change more than others, BUT we all change. If we cannot find the time to make reasoned changes in our lives, then this syndrome of being 'dead from the neck up' will not speak well for attaining any contented life. Adjustment to the external input to our minds takes time-dependent evaluation. For one thing, additional input is most often needed, and if we don't have the time to seek additional input then the resulting change in behavior and thinking will be erroneous. Much of what we regret, we never really thought through, or sought additional input for the best kind of output. Faith-based people invariably spend a lot of time saying "I don't want to talk about it". I suppose there are exceptions, but most faith based people are dead serious tunnel-visioned slaves to their faith. The stronger their faith, the shriller and more hateful they become to human diversity. Right is right, their faith is the basis for right, and discussion is closed. Faith- based individuals are trapped. If they believe A, B, C, and D, and B is admitted to be wrong at some point, on what basis can they be sure A, C, and D are still true? There is a lot at stake for them. They feel up against the all-or-none law. Of course in practice, even purists rarely, if ever, believe all they read in their inherited or adopted bible. They selectively choose what is most comfortable for them to believe and ignore the rest. AGAIN, personal contentment comes from within; NO ONE can give it to you. And this includes your ethical development. This internal development requires time for solitary contemplation.

All of us need time to research, re-arrange priorities, and fine tune understandings. Today, we also need time and reflection to filter out so much potential input that will otherwise overload our plate of contemplative matters. To spend way too much time on trivial external input is a modern day fatality. Busy as a bee at the mental reflexive level of a bee, is not a good thing. Real productive thinking and re-evaluation requires some solitude. People who just drift along with social, religious, political, or cultural norms have essentially put braces on their brains. Without alterations regarding our comprehension of our changing external input, personal contentment will be nonexistent or limited. The realities, for all of us, are constantly changing—that is the nature of evolution—and if we cannot change our perceptions of reality over time we are going to suffer mal-contentedness.

We have stated repeatedly that contentment comes from within and cannot be achieved via others giving it to you. How many parents end up feeling they gave everything they could to their children, yet their children as adults are such a discontented lot? No one can give you contentment, only a more level playing field, kindness, encouragement, patience, and good examples of behavior. In the end, always, we have to run with the ball ourselves and achieve our own state of contentment. We all, as nature dictates, have differing innate abilities. We depend on others for opportunities, fairness, encouragement, etc. Attempting to sculpt someone else to fit our own personal self-image and innate abilities is a misguided adventure.

Part of change is the loss of others precious to us. While others can be of limited value to us as we deal with these losses, for the most part our losses need to be dealt with by ourselves in solitary moments. Only we ourselves can understand the personal relationship between ourselves and the person lost to us. Only our own manipulation of our internal perceptions of life can reorganize our own mental capability to proceed in our lives without the lost loved one.

Everything that has been written above requires some solitude. This, of course, is not to say other social relationships play no role. The problem today, in American culture, is more one of providing enough solitary time to do the necessary internal mental activity required to achieve personal contentment. Not only is depending on others for your own personal contentment a wrong road, but this is often a difficult path, upon which, to switch directions. It is not suggested here that there is a fixed equation. Different people need different amounts of solitary time. Often social interactions are simply easier (less intense mental probing) than personal reflections, and thus many people take the easier alternative and reach for TV, a cell phone, internet games, online chat rooms, internet messaging/twitting to avoid any intense internal solitary reflections. Amusement, trifling conversations, social babble, etc. should never be confused with personal contentment. **WE CAN'T REACH CONTENTMENT VIA LOW GRADE INFORMATION OVERLOAD. BUSY-NESS IS NOT CONTENTMENT. OBSESSIONS OF ANY SORT ARE NOT EXERCISES IN CONTENTMENT.** No matter the obsession, whether it be money, shopping, health matters, eating, TV, sex, gambling, family matters, traveling, recreational drug use, job related work——none of these, or any other obsession leads to personal contentment. All of these, in moderation, and carried out subject to the Golden Rule, can lead to contentment. Arranging priorities is a huge part of achieving contentment. **BEING ABLE TO SAY NO TO DOING THE WRONG THING FOR SHORT TERM HAPPINESS OR GAIN IS A KEY ASPECT OF ACHIEVING PERSONAL CONTENTMENT.** We cannot arrange our priorities properly until we have taken the time to understand our own relationship to God's evolutionary process.

All of us need to consider where we get our information from. Do we ourselves seek out answers about life, or **DO WE SIMPLY LET CERTAIN OTHERS, CERTAIN GROUPS, OR INHERITED SCRIPTURE, OR INHERITED CULTURE CHOOSE FOR US WHAT WE BELIEVE**? How easy, self-serving, and lazy is it to simply conclude "of course certain others are no good—they are not like ourselves". What we all do know is that the Golden Rule is an ethical principle. Who argues against the Golden Rule as being ethical? The question about others always is, "If I were them how would I like to be treated?" This does not, in itself make others right or wrong about anything. Nor does it mean people cannot be punished or isolated when they are a danger to, or harm others. It does not mean self defense against being harmed by others is inadmissible.

MODERN GADGETS MAKE THE PEACE OF SOLITUDE MORE DIFFICULT TO OBTAIN. In my own lifetime, the time people spend in solitude has changed dramatically. When I was growing up it was easy to be bored, and we were forced to sit around, to muse about just everything, and to be creative in amusing ourselves. There certainly was no fixed schedule arranged by our parents to get us through the day with all sorts of adult supervised activities. "Be home by supper time" was often the sole structure of the day. I don't recall ever being told not to talk to strangers, to stay in my own yard. Strangers were not afraid to talk to me or reprimand me during my formative years. I learned as much from other adults as I did from my parents. Teen years represented a rapid growth towards independence and activities based upon parental involved activities grew less and less. By the time a child reached 18 they were expected to be on their own.

This is not to say the bond between parent and offspring is lost at 18, but to say that around that age the lives of the offspring and parents became distinct entities. Holidays and special events of varied sorts were exciting chances for both parties to catch up on the other's activities. Today, with modern communication devices, that child/parent umbilical bond often is never really broken. This can put strain on marriages and put limitations on the ability of an adult offspring to establish a clear separate identity, while the risk here is that the parental bonds are never really broken and an expanded family merely circles the wagons and limits interaction with others outside the family. Neighborhood social life has taken a big hit. More and more we have extended families living lives in social isolation, forever distrustful of others and diversity. If we tend to develop some irrational beliefs or paranoia about life, or others, we can always connect via modern communication methods with others having the same such paranoid leanings.

It is not all that difficult to distinguish between those who are contented and those who are not. People who are discontented complain about others a lot in very personal ways. Discontented people tend to be very rigid, seldom changing opinions or beliefs about anything. People who are discontented often feel the strongest that they 'earned' any successes and thus put down others with less success as being at fault themselves for any hardships (blame the victim). Appreciation for diversity is a rarity among the discontented. Discontented people are far more about themselves than others—they rarely get involved in any battles for rights for those without certain rights, or give time or money to causes that benefit the least amongst us. Those who focus entirely on their own search for wealth, titles, power, sexual conquests, popularity, social successes, etc, will never reach contentment. In the extremes there are people like Rush Limbaugh, evangelical ministers, Ayatollahs, Archbishops, Santorum, Terrell Owens, Brett Favre, Bill Bellichek, Bill Parcels, Putin, Donald Trump, Sarah Palin, and a high number of movie stars. There is a cruel dichotomy here—"Be careful for what you wish, you might get it." A Terrell Owens achieved an impressive amount of athletic success through sheer willpower, focus, and a singularity of purpose that the rest of us could never come close to matching—and yet, the price paid for all this is often paid in other areas of life thus neglected.

Therein lies a true life conundrum—with no such focus and sheer willpower a Terrell Owens would be just another nobody, a product of a poor formative environment, working a menial job, and so forth. But some of those nobodies may be more content later in life than a Terrell Owens. Despite what his critics hammer Terrell Owens with, there are no victims at all in his pursuit of success. He was just different and this difference was simply intolerable to those who basically resented his ability to get to the top of the mountain on his own, his own way, and brag about it every which way. He survived nearly twenty years in the NFL with good stats despite the unprecedented assault by a cabal of critics determined to stop him. If contentment was the goal, Terrell never got there. Some respect what he did, others hate him for the way he did it. In the absence of victims, I personally side with respect for his achievement. Were he to get the respect deserved for his career from most others, he then could achieve some contentment. **THE POINT HERE IS THAT SOMETIMES OTHERS CAN BE RESPONSIBLE FOR THE LACK OF CONTENTMENT SOME PEOPLE ACHIEVE.** I doubt there is any football player around who can say Terrell Owens is the reason they didn't have success in football. If Terrell Owens was the poison pill his detractors say he was then teams would have done better when he left, Tony Romo would have done better, etc. That simply was never the case. No team did better with the possible exception of Cincinnatti, at which time he was 38 years old. Probably all of us, at times, need examine why we hate the success of someone, not because they achieve success at the expense of others, but because we are irritated by their unconventional (to us) personality. The more we achieve contentment, the less likely such diversity of personality will irritate us.

We have just lived through decades in which special interest lobbyists have yielded unprecedented powers to control government officials. Lobbyist power comes through the ability to control electability of politicians. Somehow elections have become billion and million dollar processes. Lobbying has led to an accumulation of our wealth, as a country, into the hands of a small population percentage of very wealthy citizens. But the tide may be about to turn. The internet has enabled common people of all sorts to be in daily communication. People are no longer limited to TV political ads to formate their political opinions. The internet is more and more the source of where people get their news. This also means a lot of information people get is simply trash—a lot of simply unscientific, undocumented feelings about this or that. Yet the internet also provides people who really want justice, and equal rights for all, the opportunity to band together, and by their numbers, put pressure on politicians to do the right thing or lose an election. **THE LOBBYISTS MAY NOW BE MEETING THEIR MATCH**. This is a good thing. And just in time. We can hardly survive much longer with elections being won by those with millions of dollars to spend, and the 1,2, 5, or 10 percenters within striking distance of controlling virtually all three branches of our government. Not good.

We may well control our ability to be contented, with some exceptions, but without a long term understanding of the evolutionary process, it is difficult to be content in a seemingly hopeless environment. We always need to remember, that whatever the planet's status is at any present time, in the long run—so far—evolution has always been impressively progressive. In the worst case scenario, human life as those of us who now live an affluent life know it, may indeed be about to suffer a major evolutionary correction, and it could be thousands of years before a new more progressive era emerges. **BUT ALL THIS HAS NOTHING TO DO WITH WHETHER WE, AS INDIVIDUALS, CAN BE CONTENTED RIGHT NOW.**

Let's examine what our planet faces at the present time. The problems are almost all global, and this means no country can escape these problems isolated off by itself. There are no places to run, no new continents to discover, no frontiers left, less and less cultural uniqueness, etc. We are all in this together in the midst of patriotic, religious, ethnic, and economic divisions which encourage mindless intolerance and distrust/disrespect for others. Most distressing is that many of these global problems have taken years to develop and thus cannot be stopped on a dime. **MOST OF THESE PROBLEMS HAVE THEIR ORIGIN IN HUMAN OVERPOPULATION OF OUR PLANET**. Responsible reproduction is still not addressed in any serious manner. **IT IS OUR HUMAN SPECIES ACHILLES HEEL**. Below is listed an array of disturbing data which, by the number alone, should make all of us nervous. Yet we need keep in mind that just as individuals can be contented despite knowing they will die at some point near or far in time, we can still be contented individually in the face of a likely massive evolutionary correction just around the corner in our planetary history.

1. The world population has doubled since 1960. If anyone seriously thinks it can double again and things be ok, they are

logically mindless. While much of the below is a consequence of human overpopulation, none of this is listed in any particular order of importance.

2. The United States budget:

   Military (Dept. of Defense, War, Veteran Affairs, Nuclear Weapons Program)=60%
   Health and Human Services—7%
   Education—6%
   State—5%
   Other Programs—4%
   Department of Homeland Security—3.5%
   Housing and Urban Development—3%
   Justice—2%
   Agriculture—2%
   NASA—1.5%
   Energy—1%
   Labor—1%
   Treasury—1%
   Interior—1%
   Environmental Protection—1%
   Transportation—1%

"Every gun that is made, every warship launched, every rocket fired, signifies in the final sense a theft from those who hunger and and are not fed, those who are cold and are not clothed." Dwight Eisenhower.

The U.S. spends $2.1 million every single minute for war and defense.

3. By 2025, 1.8 billion people will live in regions suffering from water scarcity, and 2/3 of the global population will live under water stressed conditions.

4. In 2010 the increase in pay for average U. S. worker was 2%, for CEO's in was 23% (Average pay at the top 200 firms was 11.4 million)

5. One in every 31 adults in the U.S. is in prison or on supervised release at a cost of over $30,000/yr/prisoner—a cost which has risen 40% over the past 20 yrs. 16% of those in prison suffer from mental illness. With 5% of the world's population we house 25% of the world's prisoners.

6. Military expenditures (billions) in 2008 by various countries: U.S.—$607; China—$84.9; France— $65.7; U.K.-$65.3; Russia—$58.6; Germany—$46.8; Japan—$46.3; Italy-$40.6; India--$30. Cost to U.S. of wars in Iraq and Afghanistan since the conflicts began=$903 billion.

7. Percentage of college students who feel "down, depressed, or hopeless" is way up (recent AP/MTV survey)

8. We are now in the midst of the 6th species extinction wave in planetary history. The Permian extinction, 250 million years ago, resulted in the extinction of an estimated 70% of all terrestrial animals and 90% of all marine animals. The reign of the dinosaurs ended 65 million years ago. It is estimated that 20-30 percent of our current species will be extinct by the end of this century. One in every four mammals is currently at risk for extinction. It should be noted that past extinctions were

due to sudden physical changes in the environment by external forces while **THIS CURRENT SPECIES EXTINCTION RATE IS CAUSED BY THE ACTIVITIES OF ONE SPECIES—THE HUMAN SPECIES.** It is the nature of humans to view ourselves, as a species and as individual humans, as special favorites of God, individually important, as the God intended species to dominate all other species and to view our natural resources as unlimited. There is nothing in the long history of evolution to indicate any of this is so. The only known fact here is that the human species is just one of many species to have evolved and are one of the more recent species in evolutionary history. There is no known fact that we are a favored species nor that God is impressed with how humans treat other species or the planet's natural resources. Rather than claim we are a favored species and have dominion over all other species, we could just as well argue that God is madder than hell at human mistreatment of other species and the natural environment. There is no evidence that God's evolutionary process has ever favored any species. Instead, all the evidence indicates that it is God' evolutionary the laws which govern the process and will determine the future—and that future has nothing to do with us as individuals.

9. We, as Americans, have become so fixated on making the Middle East operate more like America that we have instead ended up making America operate more like a Middle Eastern country. Violence as a means to an end only results in violence begetting violence. Violence, unchecked, leads to chaos, and in chaotic times, thugs become the operative controlling force. Whether it is one of religious belief that God is on a particular sect's side, or a nation believing God is on its side, or an ethnic group believing God is on their side, etc.— all such beliefs lead to persecution, violence, and finally chaos. If God were really on

anyone's side this observation would have certainly been noted by history. There is no such evidence whatsoever.

10. In terms of share of federal wealth, specifically the amount of non military government aid given to foreign countries, the U.S. ranks 21st, yet the average American thinks the U.S. is way ahead of other countries in this respect. Private charities make up the majority of U.S. giving. We do, however, heavily arm many countries. It is probably our biggest industry—armaments.

11. The human cost of wars such as the Iraq War has become an ignored non issue. Aside from the physical damage to the country, we have displaced 4.5 million Iraqis, 1 in every six of their citizens. Less than 40% have access to clean water, more than 50% of children in many places have no access to school. There are 1.5 million war widows and 5 million orphans. The death toll is in the millions. These are 2008 figures but not a lot has changed over there. While the average American did not personally generate these figures, they are well aware that we lost 2500 people in the Trade Center bombing. Then, in the next breath, the average American will express resentment that the Iraqi people do not show any gratitude for what we have done for their country.

12. If marijuana were treated like alcohol and nicotine, both of the latter far more toxic and dangerous to health than marijuana, the largest revenue of the drug traffickers would dry up, the tax collected by the government be in the millions, our prison population dropped by 25%, and neighborhood gangs weakened exponentially. Almost without exception, those recreational drugs preferred by a majority of the citizens in any country, are legal, and those preferred by a minority are illegal. Some way to set up drug laws! And of course dealing with addiction to

any recreational drug via medical clinics for that purpose is dismissed for all except the wealthy.

13. Religious purists, of all ilk, believe Heaven waits for those who are saved. And saved means becoming part of a certain religious sect and practicing certain rituals, while anyone who becomes 'saved' can be eligible for Heaven. According to this kind of illogical thinking, a serial killer could become saved and go to Heaven while some of his victims, having never been saved, go to hell. Just a tad ridiculous.

14. Enough is never enough. The U.S. leads all other affluent nations in the rate at which wealth is accumulating in the hands of the very wealthy. There was a time when the very wealthy had a 90% income tax rate and huge estate taxes upon death. Not any more. Despite the fact this country had its healthiest across the board increase in economic status during this period, we are told today, and most buy into it, that the wealthy are best left to accumulate whatever they can and all that wealth trickles down to help the poor and less fortunate. If so, why are more and more falling further and further into a poor economic category while the rich get richer and richer? Where is that trickle going? Clearly the wealthy are trickling on themselves. In 2006 the top 1% averaged $1.3 million in income at an income tax rate of 22.8%. Keep in mind that the real income is hidden, exempted, tax deductible. etc. Over the past 20 years the 1% saw their share of the nation's income double, from 11.3 % to 22.1% while their tax burden shrunk by one third. In 1955 the richest 400 reported an average of $12.3 million income (2006 dollars). In 2006 the top 400 averaged $263.3 million in income and paid only 17.2% of it in tax. In 1955 those who made more than $2 million (in 2006 dollars) were taxed at just over 49%; by 2006 their tax rate had fallen to just 23.2%. Today they pay even less in taxes and

some don't pay any tax at all. When people ask how we can pay off our state and national debts the answer is common sense. It has to come from those who have most of our wealth. It certainly cannot come from the poor and the only way to get it from the middle class is to push more of them into poverty.

15. Religious Intolerance—when the penchant for using violence to resolve diversity reaches a certain level and religion gets involved the result is invariably the most horrific acts of violence imaginable. That level has been reached across the globe in more and more places. My way or the highway is well known among religious purists of differing faiths. Even in the U.S. there is this strong movement to makes certain religious beliefs the law of the land. It is all so inane. Faith-coerced is no faith at all, only tyranny. We already have our War on Drugs and all the negative impact this has on our society. Imagine if abortions became illegal, and if people gained the right to not sell something to somebody in a public store because they don't wish to use such a product themselves? With a little more effort we could have underground markets of all sorts with the accompanying gangs and violence always associated with such illegal designations. How many places in the globe already are unsafe because of religious warfare?

16. Gun Proliferation—The percentage of people in the U.S. who now carry guns legally and openly is not as high as in Iraq—YET. But it is getting there at a rapid pace. In one year 31,224 people die from gun violence. 12,632 people are murdered, 3,067 children and teens die from gun violence, and 17,352 people kill themselves. Of course, if guns didn't exist people can readily find other ways to kill each other or themselves. BUT, the ready access to a loaded gun ensures that such a decision can be made on the spur of the moment when their emotional state is over the top.

17. Climate Change—That whether the planet's climate is changing is still debated is a clear reflection of how low on the ladder science is to so many people's conclusions about important issues. We live in a modern age where beliefs and feelings have once again emerged to govern the minds of so many modern day "flat-earth" people: "I see and or feel with my own senses the answer to problems" is their mantra. It is George Bush's "in my gut I feel…." "I can see with my own eyes and feel with my own common sense that the earth is flat; therefore it is." And so it goes with climate change. That the earth's average yearly temperature is rapidly rising simply is a measured fact. Science tells us there are 3 possible reasons for this temperature rise: the sun, the earth's reflectivity, and green house gases. The verdict is in rather conclusively: green house gases as a result of human activities is the culprit. We have known this for some time. And we know the first problems will be weather extremes. We are already experiencing weather extremes in many parts of the globe and our own country. But most people could either care less to know, or choose to believe it is all a lie. One could easily go to Google and read the scientific findings, but why confuse a belief? It has taken decades, many decades, to reach this point and we may already be past the returning point. It would take decades to reverse this trend. With increasing human population and activity any reversal is rather unlikely. In fact during the dozens of Presidential debates this issue is barely, if at all, mentioned.

Chapter 22

It has always been useful for me to consider any years past 50 to be bonus years. We have, by then, with personal variations, survived our formative years and most of our productive years. The last phase, our terminational years, are best suited to the opportunity for contemplation and contentment. Contemplation is easy enough, and probably universal for everyone during this final stage of life. Contentment, however, is more complicated and comes with several caveats. If we have not engaged in protecting our health in the first two stages of life, the odds are markedly reduced that we will have good health for a long period of time in our terminational years. Poor health in our terminational years just makes substantial contentment more difficult. Perhaps it can be achieved but the hill to get there just becomes steeper.

With good health, the road is open for the contentment we have searched for all our lives. Remember, contentment is not an all or none mental state. The attainment of contentment is always one of degree. There is no claim here that some degree of contentment cannot be reached in the first two stages of life. But healthy terminational years set the stage for maximum contentment—a fitting finale to our lives. Just finishing any kind of race brings some contentment. Running a better race than the time before brings even more contentment. We have all run, in our formative and productive stage of life, many kinds of races over all sort of things. Of course, winning a race brings the most contentment. Thus, I suppose we really ought to say that **THE MEANING OF LIFE IS ALL ABOUT MAXIMIZING THE LEVEL OF CONTENTMENT WE ACHIEVE.**

So, it starts with good health in our terminational years. **WE THEN NEED TO ADD THE GRATITUDE WE FEEL FOR THE MANY BLESSINGS IN OUR LIVES**. Not blessings which God singled us out to receive, but blessings that came from a God-created evolutionary process, which gave us these blessings via chance, environment, genetics, and help from others. **WE CAN —FOOLISHLY — ELECT TO FOCUS ON THE BLESSINGS GOD'S EVOLUTIONARY PROCESS FAILED TO BESTOW UPON US**. Only a fool wins the lottery and then is angry because others have won more and bigger lotteries. Remember, enough is as good as a feast.

Next, in our terminational years, we need put all the pieces of our own life puzzle together so that we can understand ourselves. **WE NEED TO SPEND TIME IN NATURE—ALONE—TO LOOK UPON THE WONDERFUL GIFTS GOD HAS GIVEN TO ALL OF US IN SUCH A WAY THAT WILL HELP US ACTUALLY FEEL PART OF THE PROCESS WE HAVE JUST PARTICIPATED IN FOR MANY YEARS.** Our 'many years' is, of course, but a minuscule part of the whole time period for the evolutionary process. This helps us shed any self-serving feelings of special importance to the process. The reality is this: if we, by chance, had not existed, then the same purpose we may have served—sooner or later—would have been served by someone else, likewise by chance. We certainly are special in the sense that no one else like us ever existed, or will likely ever exist again. On the other hand, in a huge magnificent palace constructed with many bricks, no one brick is individually special. Since diversity drives the evolutionary process, any effort on our part to detest diversity and start placing value judgments on diversity is a very tricky game, and limits our ability to raise our own level of contentment. Rush Limbaugh is a good example. How could he possibly develop any high level of contentment when his whole mind set is focused on attacking diversity in just about every form? The man has no clue as to how the evolutionary process works.

The formative years are the most dependent stage of our lives. The productive years are the most accomplishing years of our lives. **THE TERMINATIONAL YEARS, TO BE EFFECTIVE IN MAXIMIZING CONTENTMENT, NEED TO BE OUR MOST INDEPENDENT YEARS OF OUR LIVES.** If we insist upon depending on others to amuse us, and we become a pest to others, then the terminational years are going to be bumpy and frustrating. We will feel abandoned by family, friends, God, and any others who once were such an important part of our lives. My dad used to tell my mother, "If something happens to me, don't you go live with any of your sons. They have a life to live and you won't be happy. If push comes to shove, go to a retirement home or complex of some sort and build relationships there." I thought at the time, "What a cruel thing to tell my mother, like as if her kids don't want her around." But she followed his advice and was amazingly contented until the last year of her life, and at that point her mental state was somewhat fuzzy.

Each person needs to find the time of day when he/she can feel most contemplative and most in touch with the evolutionary process. For me it is late at night, when most are asleep and everything is so quiet—the car traffic gone, the bustle of 'humanistic ants' bustling every which way gone, and all that is left is the deafening silence of the evolutionary process wending its way into the future–a future we cannot imagine, nor of which will we ever be a part—but the amazing thing is that we have been a part of the process–the size of the evolutionary part irrelevant–and the wonder of it all cements our gratefulness and admiration of life. **AFTER ALL IS SAID AND DONE, LIFE IS A CONTINUUM, AND EVERY SINGLE LIVING LIFE FORM CAME FROM LIVING CELLS**. I suppose life began sometime, somehow, but once it took hold, it never ended — with the same molecules rearranging themselves into unique and different life forms. To say that life begins at conception is just ignorance. All life ever does is change form. We may now be old, but we once were young, we once were an embryo—before that we were an egg and a sperm and each of them came from other living cells and those cells too came from other living cells and this can go back millions of years. A complete genealogy for any of us would be an extremely long document and eventually it would go back to single celled organisms.

While the Golden Rule is a globally-accepted ethical principle and active ethics the road to contentment, **THREE AREAS IN LIFE SEEM THE BIGGEST ROADBLOCKS TO THE GOAL — PATRIOTISM, RELIGIOUS SECTARIAN 'ZEALOTISM', AND 'FAMILY VALUES'**. The Holocaust and the Vietnam War are perfect examples of blind patriotism. More than two million Jews were killed and 2 million Vietnamese killed simply because of blind patriotic allegiance. It is always asked, "How could the German people have gone along with such carnage?" Less often asked is "How could the American people (including myself) have gone along with such carnage in Vietnam?." In the My Lai massacre alone, more than 500 civilian women, children, old women and men were simply rounded up, their houses burned down, the villagers shot in cold blood, and their bodies dumped along roadsides and in ditches. Dozens of soldiers were court-martialed, only one convicted and then he was pardoned by the President. The public provided the pressure for the President to pardon the convicted soldier. The participating soldiers in the massacre claimed the military and politicians were to blame, that they were just following orders. Really? So if a Muslim zealot builds a bomb, and kills some non-Muslim heathens, he is not to blame? After all, he was just following orders (in this case beliefs from on high). Again, real ethics does not depend on particular religious affiliation, political affiliation, or authoritarian decrees of any sort. And yet, too many of us, too many times, treat others differently than we would have them treat us, simply because we have misplaced loyalties. Ethics does not always come first, albeit we all know it should.

For the President, or any of us, to say "God Bless America" is really a self-serving arrogant command. We are essentially ordering God to bless America, and are quite proud of the order we have just issued. We expect our President to order God to bless us. I presume if he doesn't issue this order, God will be insulted and fail to do this blessing. Of course, somewhere in some distant land, others are commanding God to bless their own country. It might make a little more sense for us to be a bit more humble, and maybe say, "Please God, give us the strength to follow the Golden Rule in all our interactions with our fellow humans." Certainly, if we consider all humanity to be God's children, then why are we telling God to bless some and not all? In fact, on what logical basis are we telling God whom to bless? If a President fails to end an address by not ordering God to bless America, does that mean God will forget or decline to bless America? I don't think we are really calling the shots via prayers. What parent operates on the basis of "If you want me to do something nice for you or be just to you, you must beg for it."?

'Family values' cannot be used to negate the Golden Rule. 'Family values,' to many, means circling the wagons around family, basically feeling that family always comes first. 'I come first' is not part of the Golden Rule and 'my family first' is not either. On what basis do we think God would put our family first? And if God won't, then how can we justify doing just that ourselves? We should never confuse family obligations and duty with adherence to the Golden Rule.

Putting the Golden Rule first as our ethical mantra, and all the obligations and duties that come with this mantra, does not mean our loyalty and love for offspring, friends, or anyone else is diminished. It is our culture which has created a false impression of our obligations to family members. Every prophet in every religion has stressed the obligation to raise children properly, to protect them from harm, to teach them the Golden Rule, to give them good advice, to care for them when sick, to help them learn all sorts of things, to support them emotionally, and to support them financially until they are grown. They are, after all, our own creation (if I can use the term loosely)—the product of our own genes and endless developmental efforts. The hope is always that strong bonds will remain when they have become adults.

Of course every parent/grown-child relationship will be different. BUT, all adults have special obligations to each other which emanate from the Golden Rule. In a good parent/offspring relationship neither one will ever forget and will be forever conscious of the bonds established in the formative years. In time of need each should always be there for the other. But the key word here is **NEED**. Any person of adult age is responsible for their own productive years. This includes how we live our lives, the means whereby we earn our living, how we accumulate our own level of wealth, what kind of smart health choices we make, the kind of mate we chose, the kind of friends we establish, etc. **EVERY ADULT, WITH EXCESS WEALTH PAST THE BASICS NEEDED TO LIVE COMFORTABLY, IS OBLIGATED BY THE GOLDEN RULE TO SHARE THAT WEALTH WITH THE LESS FORTUNATE.** No society can last any real length of time when adults in that society fail to do this. In America we play games with this obligation, and many try to dismiss this using 'family values'. It starts with the illusionary statement of, "I earned my wealth, it is mine to do with as I wish". Somehow God's laws which govern the evolutionary process—genetics, environment, chance, and help from others—were non-existent or too minuscule to matter. With this sort of banner in hand, some then reject any obligation to return excess wealth back into the society from which they got that wealth. The attitude becomes this: the least fortunate in society can pull themselves up by their own bootstraps, just like those successful did. Socialism becomes a bad word. Sharing with the less fortunate is without any obligation. Me first. Family first. Ethnicity first. Inherited or marriage adopted religion first. Nation first.

Family first is not a bad concept if used properly. If any of our offspring, for whatever reason, become one of the least fortunate in society, then this offspring can be first in line for our charity. There is nothing in the Golden Rule which declares that the least fortunate does not apply to our own adult children. **HOWEVER**, in most cases our adult children are not among the least fortunate in society. Bus drivers may not make a salary which will make them affluent, but neither are they among the least fortunate. "Well", we might ask, "If we want to give money to one of our adult children for a mortgage down payment, why can't we if we are affluent enough to do so?" The answer is simple. We can. Let's say we are about to buy a $40,000 car. Let's assume a car to get us from place to place can be purchased for like $20,000. As stated earlier, if we buy the $40,000 car then we need match the extra $20,000 with a $20,000 dollar gift to a legitimate charity. That way, above the basics needed to live comfortably, the least fortunate count as much as ourselves. That seems fair enough. In practice this means maybe we would compromise and buy a $30,000 dollar car and give $10,000 to the less fortunate or an environmental cause, and so on. That works too. OR, maybe we want to give one of our adult children some money for a down payment on a mortgage. In that case we could opt to go with a $30,000 car and give $10,000 to one of our adult children and $10,000 to charity. The size of these figures will depend on the extent of our own economic status.

Americans are quite conflicted about all this. We say we value each person being able to make their own career and wealth, but then we also have this notion that our adult children are entitled to our excessive wealth during life or at death. These notions are in direct opposition to each other. After our children are grown our ethical duties change. In their formative years children are specifically parent responsibility. As adults in society, they are of a different status. Understanding that life is not a level playing field, that all of us have a responsibility to help level the playing field for others, that all humans are God's children via an evolutionary process that generated every one of us–understanding all this enables us to not only understand our ethical duties, but to have our ethical behavior be action orientated. **ONLY IF WE DO ALL THIS CAN WE MAXIMIZE CONTENTMENT WITH OUR LIVES.**

The notion that this sort of ethics is a lessened love for our own offspring is not valid at all. The children of Bill Gates and Andrew Carnegie understood the ethics involved and were better off for it. Remember, we cannot achieve contentment in our lives by being handed anything above that which is needed for basic living. People who receive large inheritances, and are affluent as a result, are fooling no one and certainly not themselves. This kind of practice is not harmless at all. Hoarding wealth via inheritance does irreparable harm to society. If the wealth of a society cannot be used to help the less fortunate, it cannot save the rich. We all are part of society, and we all benefit from a society in which self-sufficiency of all is maximized. We all know, for example, that poor schools affect the future prospects of children. That is exactly why we want our own children in good schools. But the Golden Rule clearly implies that, therefore, all children should be in good schools. We all know that good health care is important for everyone, not just ourselves or our own family. Yet we resist making good health care available to everyone. This is not socialism. Socialism implies we don't have to do anything and someone else will pay for our needs. Active ethics doesn't relieve anyone of responsibility; in fact, **IT REQUIRES REAL DUTIES AND REAL SACRIFICES** by the rich and poor.

The healthiest mindset for offspring is to understand that as adults they are pretty much on their own regarding their productive years. The best coaches give their best effort to train their athletes for the upcoming contest. Naturally when the contest starts, it would be unethical for a coach to give his own athletes a head start or better position for the contest. It would be unethical. For parents to help their children at all will require sacrifice as described earlier (a less expensive car, etc.). When a parent dies there would be none of the sibling battles over who gets the largess. If offspring did not expect an inheritance, the relationship between parents and offspring would be more genuine and ethical. What is ethical about creating a vulture system with inheritances? Is there anyone who really thinks God prefers us to give our wealth, upon death, to anyone except those least fortunate? And isn't it part of parental responsibility to make sure our offspring understand exactly why inheritances need be given to the least fortunate?

And let's be clear here that help for the less fortunate is always based on the concept: "Give me a fish and I eat for a day; teach me to fish and I eat for a lifetime." Providing others with good schools, good health, security, opportunities, and so on, is done to enable more people to become productive, responsible members of society. It certainly doesn't say that after we give you good schooling we will then guarantee the job you like, the salary you like, the location you like, the career you want, etc. Yet this is exactly the mentality many parents take with their children. After they have done all they can to provide the basis for success, all the parental wealth is there for their children, as adults, to squander or use to build their own pile of wealth. To top all this off, since many people live to be quite old now, the 'children' who inherit the family fortune are already past or near the end of their productive years, so why is there this need for them to have the parents money? For their health care? Everyone should be entitled to good health care and everyone should pay in enough money to ensure all have good health care. That is a societal responsibility, not a parental one, and it is not socialism. It is proper ethics.

There is still another way to view this question of where excess wealth gets distributed in society. Many personal rights are forfeited when a personal right endangers the welfare of others or an entire society. We do not have the personal right to drive 100 miles an hour on a public highway. If you have your own private road on your own property you can drive 100 miles an hour. In the absence of human overpopulation, individuals have the right to reproduce at will. In the presence of human overpopulation, this right is logically lost since the consequences to life on the planet for all species is dire. We are in this situation right now but the problem is to too hot politically to touch, so we pretty much, like lemmings, push onward toward the cliff. If anyone seriously thinks human population can afford to double again, as it has done in my lifetime, they are in deep denial of logic. Responsible reproduction becomes an absolute duty via the Golden Rule and trumps any self serving preferences.

The idea "It is my wealth, I generated it, I can do what I want with it" is another misinterpretation of reality. In general, a society functions best when there is a reasonable distribution of wealth. That does not mean individually earned wealth is wrong. But it does require that individual adults achieve their OWN pile of affluence. No society can afford to take huge portions of their collective wealth and let it become sequestered within a small percentage of the population. Our own country is faced with this situation right now and, so far, too paralyzed to do anything about it. So once again, we all lose the right, according to the Golden Rule, to take our own excess wealth and sequester it within some sort of genetic cabal. This practice is wrong for society and wrong for the individuals who receive these inheritances.

Again, we need to remember, no one can give you contentment, contentment comes from within. Thus, the notion that we can make our grown offspring contented by handing them our excess wealth is a misleading notion. Where are all these people who inherited money for their affluence who are so contented? I have been around plenty of them and learned to avoid them precisely because it was never a contented environment. These people are always fussing, and invariably about nonessential matters. Many years ago when I was a chauffeur for a very rich widow it just amazed me how unhappy the whole clan was.

They had everything and everything seemed to amount to nothing. Nobody trusted anyone else; there was little, if any, affection; conversations were superficial; and the environment was coldly calculated and competitive. What, I would ask myself, was there to compete for? They all had way more wealth than they could possibly need, so can't enough ever be enough?

It would seem, that for family relationships to be strengthened and genuine, this question of who is going to inherit parental wealth needs to be off the table. If parent and an offspring can't get along by the end of the formative years, then holding out the carrot of an inheritance hardly creates any genuine compatibility. In the last analysis, aside from the relationship between parent and offspring, excess wealth cannot be sequestered in genetic cabals **BECAUSE** it is harmful to society in general. We realized this back in the early 1900s and acted. The income tax was steeply gradated and the inheritance tax was huge. What followed were decades of prosperity for our entire society. History has shown, without exception, that if wealth is allowed to accumulate in genetic cabals, the society collapses. Always. America faces this dilemma today. 2-5% of our population owns 90% of the wealth (the figures differ a little here) and yet the wealthy want even more. That more can't come from the poor because they don't have it, and if it is taken from the middle class then more of them will be shoved into the poor category.

Thus, if we want to help our kids, including our own kids' kids and so on, then giving our kids our excess wealth, during life or at death, is a mistake. It is more than a practical mistake, it is an ethical mistake. The Golden Rule is clear enough about this issue. We all have a duty to give our excess wealth to the less fortunate, not to genetic tie-ins. In the process we can maximize our own contentedness. We not only gave our kids our best efforts for them in their formative years, and emotional support thereafter, but we helped the least fortunate amongst us on the planet. God's evolutionary process gave humans the ability to help each other according to our needs, and if we don't use this potential, then we cannot reach full contentment, and those less fortunate will not be helped. **WE CANNOT, IN ESSENCE, PRAY FOR GOD TO HELP THE LESS FORTUNATE WHEN WE WILL NOT**. We need repeat this to ourselves over and over until, in our mind, it is set in stone.

In a practical sense, many elderly are helped considerably by offspring, relatives, or others essentially because the 'helpers' realize an inheritance will be forthcoming. Thus, we could conclude "at least they got help". True, but the same help could come from others who are willing to do it out of sense of ethical duty and by the government via the collective contribution from all citizens. There are three ways to help those less fortunate or in need. First, the government can be there with a 'safety net'. This works best in matters of health care, housing, meal on wheels, education, etc. Second, those with excess wealth can use that excess wealth to help the less fortunate. Third, those without excess wealth can contribute time to assist those with needs. Thus, most people can help those in need in some form or fashion. Those less fortunate need to register their needs and the government can set up register centers to process these needs and screen volunteers to meet these needs. This means an elderly person can still, of course be helped out by their offspring, other relatives, and friends out of loyalty, kindness, pay back, ethical duty — whatever. Most of us are not going to take the attitude, "Let others help mom in her latter years with errands, visits, etc. because there is nothing in it financially for me." It is not likely anyone benefits from disingenuous 'assistance'. To even view that sort of family interaction is painful and sad. Neither party is happy. The recipient knows that the 'assistance' is done begrudgingly and the giver is 'no happy camper' providing the assistance.

I suppose, in some sense, this means parents take full control and responsibility to meet the needs of their children while all of society has the responsibility to meet the needs of the less fortunate. The Golden Rule does not nullify 'family values', it just redefines 'family' and clears up our responsibilities to whom when. Were the Golden Rule to be seriously followed as a widespread ethical duty there would be no homelessness, no one attending a poor school, no one starving, no one without good health care, no one without an opportunity to work at the level of their capability—and of course that includes our own offspring. The last statement needs clarification. Everyone has an obligation to be productive at something in life, commensurate with their abilities. If they decline to do so, society is not obligated to assist them. Free loaders do not qualify. There is nothing about the Golden Rule which implies otherwise. Thus, an elderly person who is still mobile cannot sign up to have her groceries delivered, for example. There may be shady areas but for the most part needs are pretty clear cut.

The least advantaged can be helped in life by a change in environment, a change in opportunity, a change in the quality of education, and a change in the quality of health. While those affluent can use their excess wealth to support the least advantaged directly, or through charitable organizations, efforts must also be made to support those politicians whose policy positions favor government help to the least advantaged. This is especially true in health care, in education, in equal opportunity laws, in tax laws, in estate tax laws, in equal rights, in minimum wage levels, in college loans, etc. If a person does not have money, they can find time to help elect politicians who will do the most to help the least advantaged.

In the best scenario, no one need worry about whether they have money to care for their health care. This is a responsibility of every government; that is to say everybody in every country has an ethical obligation—collectively, to see to it that all citizens have good schooling and good health care. Those who push the hardest to get government off the people's back and let individuals control their own destiny are almost, without exception, people whose own affluence is such that they can well afford good health care and to live in neighborhoods which can afford excellent schools. In other words, the hell with the less fortunate.

There is still another area almost totally ignored by society. Besides good health care and good schools, every child needs quality peers and adults in their formative years. There would be nothing wrong, and everything right, about a government which tracks every child in this respect. If a child is in need of quality 'uncles' 'aunts', 'grandparents', 'cousins', etc., then there needs to be a mechanism whereby others can volunteer to be any of these to a child in need. Responsible reproduction, at this point in history, necessitates limited natural offspring, but the opportunities to be volunteer 'uncles', 'aunts' 'grandparents' and 'cousins' would be endless. Who, we might ask, would determine who is qualified to be any of these to a child in need? Well, we license people to be all kinds of things and there is no real reason why government can't license people who volunteer in this capacity. We all have known others who have reached out personally to be such 'step-whatevers' to youngsters in need. What we need is for this to be relatively common, not rare. No attempt is made here to go into any great detail.

Even if a particular country were to get its act completely together and develop a culture based on the Golden Rule, there will still be other areas of the world where people need food, housing, health care, security, education, etc. Thus, a lot of money we might donate to charity will go to these people, wherever they might be. There is absolutely no need, in reality, why anyone anywhere should be starving, homeless, or without help to cure a curable disease. Only the failure of humans to adopt the Golden Rule as our planetary ethic prevents this. Through His evolutionary process God has given us the ball. We need to run with it.

So, we can ask, "Who will pay the bill?" This is simple: excess wealth, during life or upon death, and altered priorities in government spending. The amount of money available from these sources is vast and more than enough to do the job. This obsession with capitalism, dictatorship, socialism, communism—whatever—is distracting. The only prerequisite for society is to have the Golden Rule be the cultural norm, the ethical standard. Wherever this prevails, government structure, in any form, is tailored to this cultural standard. My own preference is capitalism with regulations and limits. This maximizes personal commitment to self improvement.

There is no escape from sacrifice. No matter how much, for example, we may understand that our excess wealth needs to go to the less fortunate, this competes with the natural desire to spend it on ourselves and our offspring. Sloppy sorriness for the less fortunate is not sufficient. With modern communication devices we cannot plead ignorance of the plight of others. We see these people on TV, in magazines, on internet videos, in books about them and so on. We are obligated to help. The Golden Rule demands it. But how can we help? We are limited as individuals. We could, I suppose, actually locate and intercede on behalf of a particular example of the least fortunate. But even reaching them would be difficult. If we ourselves are affluent, the likelihood of us ever happening upon the least fortunate is slim. We are not likely to be found wandering in the ghettoes, refugee camps, war ravaged neighborhoods, homeless shelters, etc. When is the last time any of us affluent ever took a stroll through any of these areas—even the poorest (and most dangerous) segments of Newark, Chicago, Los Angeles, New Orleans, etc.—let alone any foreign, even worse, counterparts? Indeed, many affluent actually preach freedom from government regulations—the old demand for individual freedom from government intervention in their lives. These are the people who strongly feel that what they have is theirs, and they should be entitled to amass as much wealth—of course with endless government tax loopholes for them to easily do this—and that when all the wealth is piled higher and higher, it then becomes an inheritable treasure for their offspring. In others words, once they have themselves extracted considerable wealth it will never be shared, let alone returned to the society from which it was derived, and certainly never available to those most in need. So who then exactly, is to help the less fortunate? I guess individual acts of charity.

Let's look at this individual act of charity a bit closer. Let's say we individually decide to help just one of these less fortunate individuals, especially the children born with few good cards in their hand. I guess we then sort of venture into one of these sorry ass places and in some sense snatch some poor child to help. This child has no good school. Are we going to build a school and staff it for the child? Are we going to build, staff, and financially support a medical care center for this child? Are we going to fix this child's teeth, find good peer friends with which the child can associate? And what about the child's parents, if the child has any—are we going to do the same for them or just help the child?

Or do we tell the parent(s), 'Look, you are in no position to raise this child, I need to adopt him/her and take him/her away from this environment'.

Clearly this Robin Hood approach to helping the less fortunate has limitations which approaches futility. In reality, this reduces us to sloppy sorriness. We can donate some canned goods, or make a small donation to groups that send the less fortunate blankets, food, emergency medical care, etc. When all this is done, some of these less fortunate remain alive to suffer future hopelessness. And of course we pray for them, sometimes alone, and sometimes en masse. God's process of evolution has given humans the ability to collectively help those less fortunate, but we often decline and ask God to do what we have the collective ability to do. What are we saying to God other than "Look, you take care of these less fortunate; we have personal materialistic desires and goals, plus our own families which we care deeply about, and our obligation is to take care of our own family today, tomorrow, and in the future". God's answer to such breach of ethical human duty is clear enough. He doesn't seem to pay much attention to these prayerful orders. God gave us the solution but we too often decline to act.

Where does all this really leave us as individuals? Clearly the Lone Ranger approach has serious limitations. Thus the question remains, "How can an effective collective response be obtained?" Organized religion has certainly not been the answer and often is a major part of the problem. I think we have seen enough of the Catholics and Protestants in Ireland, the Muslims and the Jews in the Middle East, the Muslims and Christians in Africa, the Sunni and Shiites in Iraq, etc. All of this simply reminds us of exactly why the forefathers of our own government insisted on separation of Church and State—why George Washington stated

"Ours is not a Christian government", and why Lincoln never joined a Church.

History and science have led us to a global economy. Unfortunately, a global economy without global minimum wages is self destructive. The pressure is thus there to favor slave minimum wages for workers. Not good. But that is another treatise. Now we need a global cultural ethic based on the Golden Rule. Yes, we are indeed 'our brother's keeper'. **THE ETHICS OF HOW ADULTS RESPOND TO THE NEEDS OF OTHERS LESS FORTUNATE TRUMPS ALL OTHER PERSONAL COMMITMENTS TO SELECT OTHERS WHO HAPPEN TO BE OUR OFFSPRING OR FRIENDS, WHATEVER.** While we cannot individually save the less fortunate, we can vigorously support politicians who see our government as the collective force, on behalf of all of us, to support the less fortunate everywhere. To the extent governments across the globe adopt the cultural ethics of the Golden Rule, the least fortunate will find the playing field more level. Then all kids will have good schools to attend, all people will be entitled to good health care, all people will have proper retirement benefits, all people will be required to practice responsible reproduction, all people will be provided opportunity for jobs with living wages matching the skills of the job.

Let us be able to realize that active ethics, based on the Golden Rule, is not only the answer to our personal contentment, but to the ability of the less fortunate to have a more level field in which to pursue their own contentment. It is the best of all solutions—a win/win for everyone. There is no us versus them, but everyone acting in the best interests of each other based on ethics which requires sacrifice, priorities, and a pursuit of understanding ourselves and the God created process of evolution, of which we have been blessed to be a part.

Let us understand that ethics is a human genetic trait, not based on any college degrees, any religious titles, any inherited religion, any ethnic category, any regional location, or any kind of government structure. Ethics, like any other genetic trait, is a personal potential in all of us requiring development via reason and **PRACTICE**. We are truly a part of a most amazing evolutionary process, and part of contentment is learning about that process in order that we can, to the best we can, feel a genuine part of the process. If we don't understand this process we can't go with it. If we fail to get our priorities in order, we travel the wrong path. If we can't appreciate diversity we are doomed to be angry.

Finally, nothing written in this book is written in stone. We are all unique individuals and need to tweak all this to make it conform to our own individuality. As long as we understand the Golden Rule we will know how and to what extent we can tweak any of this. And in the end, let none of us fail to acknowledge and appreciate just how much of any 'success' we may have had in any aspect of our lives is beholden to the many others in our lives who helped us along the way. Life is no normal poker game where you get certain cards in your hand and have to play them all by yourself. Others give us insight, others give us cards to add to our hands, and our chances of winning something go up. And those who were dealt the best hands and shared advice and cards with others, get to achieve contentment for their efforts to make the playing field more level for the least fortunate. The object in this game, via our species inherited ethical potential, is to let God's rules of evolution, with diversity, chance, genetics, and environment, play out, BUT ALSO to enable the least 'fit' to achieve less suffering and more contentment. Everybody can be a winner.

To many, this idea of a global culture based on the Golden Rule rather than an assortment of secular religions is simply poppycock. I would be hard pressed to disagree. There is no sign at all that humans are remotely committed globally to responsible reproduction. So human overpopulation will continue. There is no sign at all that human societies are about to stop the growing disparity between the wealthy and the poor. No matter what the form of government, the wealthy are piling up more and more of their society's wealth higher and higher. There is no sign families are much closer today to any real understanding that accumulated wealth by individuals is to be shared with the least fortunate in life, during life and/or at death. There is a disconnect between our understanding of 'God's children' and our own children to the extent we cannot yet accept that God would want the least fortunate in His evolutionary process to receive our excess wealth before any of our own offspring or other persons who are not among the less fortunate. It would be hard for us to precisely define 'God's children'. In one sense all species are 'God's children' and it is a mistake for us to assume we are more precious or have any right to abuse other species or even our natural resources (which perhaps are His 'children' too). President Kennedy once said that, "If a free society cannot help the many who are poor, it cannot save the few who are rich". In the context here we could modify that to read, "If the affluent cannot share their wealth with the less fortunate, they cannot save their own offspring."

In global ethics, based on the Golden Rule, the responsibilities for ethics is shared between government and individuals. We cannot, for the most part, individually create a level playing field for the less fortunate, or protect other species, or protect our environment. It is a responsibility for government, of any kind, to force all its citizens—at least affluent citizens—to share their wealth with the less fortunate. It is government which can level the playing field for education, for health care, basic job and salary standards, basic food and shelter needs—things of this sort. It is government which ensures that depriving any group of their human rights is punishable by law.

It is our individual responsibility to support the right government leaders and policies. If we don't, we are guilty of, at best, disingenuous ethics. It makes little ethical sense to show apoplectic concern for unborn embryos with no human personalities or memories—and then support policies which allow children in poor neighborhoods to have inferior quality schools or inferior health care. This is simply unethical.

While the affluent have the ethical obligation to share their excess wealth with the less fortunate through worthy charities, all individuals can share some of their time to help the less fortunate. We can all help supply worthwhile charitable causes with the manpower to effectuate their goals. We can all help out where needed to become 'uncles, aunts, grandfathers, and grandmothers to children in such need. To facilitate this kind of help the government can help identify who the children are with such needs.

Finally, it is both the government and individuals who have an ethical responsibility to ensure responsible reproduction to protect humanity, other species, and natural resources from human overpopulation.

Admittedly, time is about running out for all the above to happen today, or in the near future. So what will happen? While the particulars may be debatable and unpredictable, God's laws of nature dictate that human population will be controlled. Among the candidates to do the job are disease; nuclear war; chemical war; biological war; cosmic events; barbaric chaos for food, water and other resources; climate change; and so on. And I suppose, as a long shot, maybe humans will find a new suitable planet elsewhere for a new frontier. Sounds crazy, but then again humans took several months to reach the American continents early on, and maybe several months in space travel would bring us to a new planet for our new frontier. But enough; we are better at understanding the past than the future.

Total extinction of the human species would seem unlikely. Our advanced brainpower might prevent this. Perhaps the lessons learned will bring about the needed ethical Golden Rule revolution to human society. We have driven many species to extinction at a rate almost unheard of in the evolutionary process. Interestingly, we also seem close scientifically to being able to bring some of these species back.

Something, it seems, is going to give—and not too far down the road.

If the reader wishes to read an excellent description of the evolutionary process by a professional in the field I recommend "The Greatest Show On Earth" by Richard Dawkins. This is a very readable and insightful examination of the evolutionary process.

If the reader wishes to read a more professional discourse on these philosophical issues you can't go wrong with Peter Singer or Sam Harris. "The Moral Landscape" by Sam Harris is especially effective in demonstrating how reason can be used to dictate ethics.

I will close this book with two quotations. The first attempts to put in perspective my own method for tackling the topic. The second is a quotation, whose source I can't seem to pinpoint, but is one I use often to close my thoughts on a contented life.

"It is commonplace of all religious thought, even the most primitive, that the man seeking visions and insight must go apart from his fellows and live for a time in the wilderness. If he is of the proper sort, he will return with a message. It may not be a message from the God he set out to seek, but even if he has failed in that particular, he will have had a vision or seen a marvel, and these are always worth listening to and thinking about...... One must seek, then, what only the solitary approach can give–a natural revelation." Loren Eiseley (Anthropologist, philosopher, natural science writer, sometimes called 'the modern Thoreau')

"There is a way of life, a way of thinking, of behaving towards other men and your fellow creatures, towards all living things, towards the whole earth and the sky and the sun that is based on love, on compassion, on respect, on cherishing everything there is around you because it is wonderful, unique, it's natural and good and it evolved that way by itself, it's got to be cherished and if we think like that, and live that kind of life, we can all have our freedom, we can all have our happiness, we can all feel the sun and smell the grass and smell the flowers and look upon each other with appreciation." (Unknown)

For additional shorter musings by this author on various topics the reader is directed to the following URL: rsjlifemusings.blogspot.com

In the absence of any unexpected change in the financial status of the author all of the financial gain from this book will be distributed to various 501 charitable organizations.

Epilogue

The basic treatise in this book, that achieving a degree of contentedness is the meaning of our individual lives, does have come caveats. For example, let us take individual X.

Individual X meets the basic criteria in this book for following the Golden Rule—giving money to charitable causes, directly helping some of the least fortunate in life, being, for the most part, a good parent, spouse, an honest, personable, caring person. And because of all this they have a degree of contentedness about themselves and their life. Goal achieved.

However, let's say Individual X dies and leaves most of their acquired wealth to their offspring. This clearly goes against the Golden Rule and against most every major prophet in every major religion. We know, for example, that Jesus said, "It would be easier for a camel to pass through the eye of a needle than for a rich man to enter the kIngdom of Heaven". Still, they are dead now and had achieved a relatively contented state. Remember, the level of contentment is not easily measured, nor need this really be necessary. So where does this leave individual X with the treatise of this book?

We need remember that according to the treatise in this book, no individuals are the center of the evolutionary process. There probably is no Heaven or Hell. We must also keep in mind that most people really want their offspring to be successful and have a good life. And we also are aware that many good people believe in the Golden Rule and also Heaven after death.

It is easy to see that not giving their excess wealth to the least fortunate, but to others, is in violation of their own religious scripture. Clearly there is no way to know which violations of scripture, to what degree, deny a person entrance to the Heaven of their scripture.

That leaves us to address the Golden Rule principle of ethics, as delineated in this book. Certainly, if any of us were among the least advantaged in society, we would want the affluent to help us out with their excess wealth—during life, and via inheritance. This is the only way to do unto the least advantaged what we would have them do for us were the situations reversed. Individual X, therefore, has also failed the Golden Rule. BUT, one could argue, so what? Individual X is dead now and achieved a contented life via the Golden Rule. They beat the system while still giving their accumulated wealth to their offspring instead of the least advantaged.

But did they? We prate on and on about how we want to leave a good life for our kids. Yet we don't hesitate to wage war by borrowing the money to do so, we run up the national debt for a lot of differing reasons and leave that debt to our offspring to pay. We need always remember this: most every major civilization in history has collapsed because of an ever increasing disparity of wealth between the affluent and the poor, plus/or a foreign 'empire' of various sorts that grew too expensive to maintain.

Thus, **all the affluent who give their wealth to affluent offspring cabals, doom their nation's offspring by that very action.** Their offspring do not live in a bubble. It is just another example of '"all that glitters is not gold". We also know from history, whenever society implodes from this insatiable accumulation of wealth among these genetic cabals, that the 'Have Nots' always win over the 'Haves'. The Have's have a lot to protect and the Have-Nots have nothing to lose.

There can be no mistake about it, whenever we contribute to this massive unearned accumulation of wealth among the already affluent, including affluent offspring, we are sealing the fate of that society down the road. **Giving our wealth to others than the less fortunate dooms the future for the very people we want to help. A healthy society enriches every component of a society.**

We also need remember that it is the role of any legitimate form of government to not let this happen. The welfare of everyone is always more important than the welfare of any component of society. At one time in our history the government did stop this accumulation of unearned wealth, and the biggest growth in standard of living for everyone followed. Through huge inheritance taxes and steep progressive income taxing, this accumulation of wealth in affluent cabals was stopped. **Earning wealth is admirable, hoarding it in genetic cabals via unearned gifts is detrimental to society.**

And let us not forget that Individual X would have been more contented in life had they willed their inheritance to the least fortunate. Some might say, "Why is it necessary for the least fortunate to get all these handouts?" At least the right word is being used—'handout". Let the question be reversed. Why should genetics play a role in who get's handouts? The solution is that

the least fortunate, in most cases, are less in need of a handout than a level playing field. Remember, every child, according to the Golden Rule Ethic deserves a good education, a good environment in which to spend their formative years, and good health care. Every adult needs good health care, decent job benefits, a decent pension or social security benefits, a living wage job, protection from discrimination and so on. None of this can be achieved, this leveling of the playing field, without the accumulated wealth of the affluent being pumped back into the society at large to level the playing field. **There is no other way to ensure a better life for the least fortunate in the absence of this directed use of accumulated wealth.**

To put it bluntly, **the government should not permit this accumulated wealth to be secured in affluent cabals**, and the rest of us individually should, for ethical reasons, do our part, whether forced to or not. Giving affluent (not the least fortunate) an inheritance does not make them contented. Contentment comes from within and need be earned. On the other hand, **giving an inheritance back into society to be used to level the playing field ensures that the future will have a society in which all socio-economic groups prosper.**

We do not live in a world of evil vs good. We are part of a process, controlled by the Creator's rules, which enables an amazing diversity of life to prosper and advance over eons of time. Individual X did not get away with anything. They did a lot of good via the Golden Rule while they lived and were rewarded right here on earth for that dedication. Individual members of any species are not perfect, and these imperfections are corrected by the evolutionary process through diversity, chance, and environment. Almost all Americans realize, right now, that buying products made by slave labor is harming our own work force here at home.

Almost all of us, including myself, realize that buying just about everything from the internet is hurting local retail businesses. We often know the right but fail nevertheless. **Sometimes, for most individuals to change, the culture must change.**

However, according to the treatise promoted by this book, all these imperfections, over time, get sorted out by the evolutionary process, and we might predict, that weak human ethical practices will be improved as TIME marches on. We are better today, as a species, with ethics than we were a thousand years ago. Humans are going to pay a price for any lack of responsible reproduction (overpopulation), just as we will for not doing a better job of leaving our excess wealth, upon death, to the least fortunate so the least fortunate can have a more level playing field. If we are not always just, the evolutionary process is, and will always operate in the best interests of the process and not any single member of any species. It takes special people to be ahead of their own culture at their time. **For us to focus on any limitations of Individual X is to lose sight of the forest for the sake of the trees.**

Life is not about specific individuals going to a Heaven or a Hell but about evolutionary progress. Specie failures, such as irresponsible reproduction and failure to return wealth earned back into the society from which it came to help level the playing field for the least fortunate—these kind of group failures—will be corrected by the evolutionary process. And the genesis for evolutionary progress in these areas will be made by individuals willing to lead the way in changing the culture that allows irresponsible behavior to thrive.

INDEX

The substantive basis for this book has been derived from the 'thoughts' of many others including the following who are identified in the book.

Aaron, Hank, 162
Acheson, Dean, 47
Adams, John, 91
Addams, Jane, 47
Adams, Cindy, 37
Allen, Woody, 118
Amiel, Henri Frederic, 60
Anthony, Susan, 42
Antonius, Marcus Aurelius, 64
Aristophanes, 118
Aristotle, 64
Arnold, Matthew, 123
Aronosfsky, Darren, 94
Ashley-Pitt, 58
Auber, Daniel-Francois-Esprit, 120
Auden, Wystan Hugh, 106, 124
Bachmann, Michele, 162
Bacon, Francis, 23
Bacon, Roger, 24
Baldwin, James, 108
Bankhead, Tallulah, 157
Barrie, James Matthew, 46, 53
Battista, Orlando, 143
Beecher, H.W., 81
Bell, Clive, 91
Bellichek, Bill, 227
Berenson, Bernard, 99
Beta, Toba, 157
Bierce, Ambrose, 11
Bird, David, 157
Bonds, Barry, 162

Bovee, C.C., 17
Brasshares, Ann, 110
Brown, Rita Mae, 97
Browning, Robert, 92
Bruce, Lenny, 94
Buddha, 27, 74, 87, 127, 128, 130
Bush, George W,, 236
Callahan, Daniel, 120
Carey, Art, 32(2), 33
Carlin, George, 98, 157
Carlyle, Thomas, 99
Carnegie, Andrew, 143, 162
Carter, Hhodding, 143
Cary, Joyce, 23
Cash, Johnny, 98
Chanel, Coco, 98
Christ, Jesus, 27, 87, 88, 127, 128, 130, 132, 164, 181, 188, 191, 216
Cicero, Marcus Tullius, 118
Clay, Henry, 18
Clinton, Hillary, 95, 107
Coffin Jr., Willam Sloane, 107
Coleridge, Samuel Taylor, 80
Colton, C.C., 32, 92
Confucius, 24, 25, 41
Cova, John, 25
Cree Indian Saying, 45
Cuomo, Nario, 37
Dawkins, Richard, 8, 259
D'holbach, Paul Henri Thiry Caron, 15, 24, 64

Diderot, Denis, 92
Disraeli, Benjamin, 80
Dobson, James, 119
Dreiser, Theodore, 93
Driberg, Tom, 64
Dubos, Rene, 106, 120
Dylan, Bob, 101
Einstein, Albert, 84, 93
Eisely, Loren, 260
Eisenhower, Dwight, 162, 230
Eliot, George, 44
Emerson, Ralph Waldo, 97, 100, 124, 125
Empedocies, 8
Epictetus, 118
Ertz, Susan, 57, 94, 108
Fields, J.T., 24
Fierstein, Harvey, 98
France, Anatole, 80
Franklin, Benjamin, 37, 61
Freud, Sigmund, 56, 118
Gandhi, Mohandas K., 27, 47, 87, 127, 128, 130
Gibbs, Sir Philip, 44
Gitt, Josiah William, 99
Goldwater, Barry, 36, 1112, 157
Graham, Billy, 162
Gray, Thomas, 30
Grellet, Stephen, 45
Griswold, Alfred Whitney, 24
Guest, Edgar A., 34
Hailsham, Lord, 64
Harris, Sam, 23(2), 259

Harris, Sydney, 25(2), 34, 46(2), 99, 124
Heraclitus, 43
Hergesheimer, Hoseph, 15
Hillel, 43
Hitler, Adolph, 12, 61, 162, 213
Hobbes, Thomas, 119
Hoch, Edward, 43
Houston, Rachael, 107
Hubbard, Elbert, 81
Hughes, Langston, 80
Hugo, Victor, 119
Hume, John, 107
Husky, Ferlin, 119
Huxley, Aldous, 24
Huxley, Thomas Henry, 93, 124
Ingersoll, Robert G., 47
James, Oliver, 97
James, William, 80
Jefferson, Thomas, 16, 42, 93, 94, 108
Johnson, Samuel, 15, 22, 157
Joplin, Janice, 125
Joseph, Ola, 107
Jung, Carl Gustav, 31, 43
Kant, Immanuel, 16, 83, 96
Kaufmann, Walter, 16
Kennedy, John F., 81, 107
Keynes, John Maynard, 17
Kierkegaard, Soren, 31
King, Martin Luther, 65
Kinnock, Neil, 47
Koppel, Ted, 56

Lama, Dalai, 27
Lamont, Corless, 16
Lee, Bruce, 98
Leno, Jay, 139
Limbaugh, Rush, 162, 226
Lincoln, Abraham, 23, 35, 42, 160, 170 187 190, 191
Lippman, Walter, 36, 99
Longfellow, Henry Wadsworth, 42
Lowell, James, 16
Lucretius, 30
Maeterlinck, Maurice, 16, 17
Marx, Carl, 42
Masssinger, Philip, 63
Mencius, 25
Mill, John Stuart, 12, 43, 105
Milne, A.A,, 98
Milton, John, 124
Mohammed, 87, 130
Monod, Adolphe, 44
Montaigne, Michael de, 125
Monthelant, Henry de, 23
Muir, John, 33
Niebuhr, Reinhold, 45
Nietsche, 45, 97, 108, 119,
Obama, Barack, 162
Owens, Terrell, 95, 227
Palin, Sarah, 162, 227
Parcels, Bill, 227
Pavlova, Anna, 31
Pears, Iain, 125
Peter, Laurence J., 32

Planck, Max, 24
Plato, 79
Powell, Anthony, 42
Reagan, Ronald, 18
Reinhardt, Stephen, 120
Reinhardt, Uwe E., 33
Richards, R.D., 54
Robertson, Pat, 162
Rochefoucauld, Francois De La, 43
Roddenberry, Gene, 107
Rodgers, Will, 12
Roosevelt, Theodore, 45(2), 48(3), 81
Root, Eilihu, 25
Ruskin, John, 81
Russell, Bertrand, 16, 42, 94
Russell, George, 43
Sachs, A., 17
Sagan, Francoise, 37
Sallust, 64
Schopenhauer, Arthur, 94
Scottish Proverb, 81
Seneca, Lucius Annaeus, 119(2)
Smiles, Samuel, 46
Sockman, Ralph W., 46
Socrates, 17
Stein, Gertrude, 30
Stevenson, Robert Louis, 31
Store, Anthony, 221
Swift, Jonathan, 18, 44
Tennyson, Alfred Lord, 2

Thomas, D., 25
Thoreau, Henry David, 32, 45, 53, 56
Tomlin, Lily, 58
Trump, Donald, 162, 227
Twain, Mark, 92
Vanderbilt, William Henry, 80
Virgil, 119
Von Goethe, Johann Wolfgang, 43
Washington, Booker T., 44
Watta, Ethel, 116
Wesley, John, 46
Winfrey, Oprah, 98
Whitehead, Alfred North, 24
Whitman, Walt, 56
Wilde, Oscar, 99
Wise, Stephen S., 35
Wolfe, Thomas, 44
Wordsworth, William, 30(2), 57
Wylie, Philip, 94
Young, edward, 32, 81

www.ingramcontent.com/pod-product-compliance
Lightning Source LLC
Chambersburg PA
CBHW061427040426
42450CB00007B/931